TWAYNE'S WORLD LEADERS SERIES

EDITORS OF THIS VOLUME

Arthur W. Brown

Baruch College, The City University

of New York

and

Thomas S. Knight

Adelphi University

Ernst Cassirer

TWLS 61

Ernst Cassirer

ERNST CASSIRER
Philosopher of Culture

By SEYMOUR W. ITZKOFF
Smith College

TWAYNE PUBLISHERS

A DIVISION OF G. K. HALL & CO., BOSTON

Library of Congress Cataloging in Publication Data

Itzkoff, Seymour W.
  Ernst Cassirer.

  (Twayne's world leaders series)
  Bibliography: p.193-95.
  Includes index.
  1.   Cassirer, Ernst, 1874-1945.   I.   Title.
B3216.C34I87   193   76-41200
ISBN O-8057-7712-1

To Edee and the Memory of Tom

Contents

About the Author

Seymour W. Itzkoff received his B.A. in music and social science from the University of Hartford, his M.A. in philosophy from the Graduate Faculty of Columbia University and the Ed.D in the philosophy of education from Teachers College, Columbia University. He is Professor of Education at Smith College, where he has taught since 1965. Before that, he taught at Hunter College, C.U.N.Y. His visiting appointments have been at New York University, Adelphi University, University of Massachusetts, and Trinity College. In addition to many articles in various scholarly journals, he has published three books: *Cultural Pluralism and American Education*, 1969; *Ernst Cassirer: Scientific Knowledge and the Concept of Man,* 1971; *A New Public Education,* 1976.

Preface

In an age when few objective standards and truths remain unquestioned, the philosophy of Ernst Cassirer reminds us of an era that was and someday must be again. He participated in the last great advances in our understanding of scientific knowledge and cultural thought that brought us up to World War II and the holocaust. As one reads in Cassirer's extensive corpus of writings, it is impossible not to be awed by his vast knowledge of contemporary physics and mathematics, ethnology, linguistics as well as history and the arts. For Cassirer, this was not an accidental accumulation of information, a mere ornament of the traditional Continental academic philosopher.

Cassirer recognized early in his own period of maturation at the turn of the twentieth century that his was a revolutionary era in the sciences as well as in humanistic scholarship. To be able to deal intellectually with these advances, he studied the materials at first hand. So well did he achieve his goal to study the past as a means of guiding our knowledge of the present that he became one of the preeminent contributors to the theory of knowledge.

The weight of his writings helped to bring the tradition of Immanuel Kant well into our century. Cassirer's neo-Kantianism resulted in both a reinterpretation of scientific knowledge and a theory of cultural experience. In one sense, his work is the realization of Kant's own philosophical program, an outline of a philosophical anthropology.

World War II shattered Cassirer's hopes to focus this knowledge on contemporary events as a guide to the future. He was driven from his homeland by the Nazis, wandered Europe for a number of years before settling in the United States. He died at the end of World War II at the beginning of a new era. If his neo-Kantian philosophy did not develop to become a dominant intellectual force, the achievements of this view of knowledge were diffused in a variety of scientific and humanistic disciplines as widely separated as physical theory, linguistics, and aesthetics.

I first encountered Cassirer in a course in aesthetics in which figured the writing of his follower, Susanne Langer. In a philosophical climate in which logic and ordinary language usage dominated all discussions, it was a revelation to find a scholar deeply immersed in the problem of scientific knowledge, culture, and human thought. The question of symbolic form penetrated into the most mysterious issues of human existence.

Yet Cassirer's work struck me as completely modern and empirical in its scope. His language in translation or in the original is difficult. This has led some mistakenly to search for any nineteenth century metaphysics that might be lurking in the corpus of Cassirer's writings. One wishes that, for the sake of popularization, his writing could have been simpler.

His ideas are complex, but he did create a new synthetic view of the relationship of the various forms of knowing in human culture. He tried also to relate this perspective to the historical tradition. Cassirer also tried to point it to the function in terms of the questions and research to which future scholars in a variety of disciplines would have to address themselves.

In this book on Cassirer's philosophy of culture, I have attempted to link the historical origins of Cassirer's neo-Kantianism to his own developing frame of reference. The major focus is on his *magnum opus, The Philosophy of Symbolic Forms*, and its basic outlook on cultural knowledge. This series of volumes was completed in 1929. Implicit in it was a theory of human nature and a host of issues tantalizing in their implications, if incomplete in their development.

I have tried to indicate in the final chapters of this book some of the implications and questions involved in this philosophy of culture. My own work, for the most part in the philosophy of education, is a reflection of the basic Kantian orientation of this philosophy. To deal with such problems, I found it necessary to add a pragmatic instrumental dimension. Cassirer would himself have been sensitive to this need. That we should apply the richness of Cassirer's own research to the tangible questions of social and cultural policy goes without saying. We need to further his basic research into the problems of symbolic knowledge and the cultural forms of experience. Susanne Langer's work in aesthetics and the theory of mind, the work of Noam Chomsky and the psycholinguists operating out of the same Continental philosophical framework, is another manifestation of the fertility of this perspective.

Preface

It is my hope that this book will stimulate students of philosophy to go back to the original writings of Cassirer and experience his richness and depth at first hand.

SEYMOUR W. ITZKOFF

Northhampton, Mass.

Chronology

1874   Ernst Cassirer born on July 28 in Breslau (now Wroclaw, Poland) into an upper middle-class Jewish family.

1896   Arrives in Marburg (Marburg University) to pursue graduate study in philosophy with Hermann Cohen.

1899   Receives his doctorate, with a thesis on Descartes' theory of knowledge.

1902   Marries first cousin, Toni Bondi, in Vienna. Publishes his first major work, *Leibniz' System in seinen wissenschaftlichen Grundlagen (Foundations of Leibniz' Philosophical System)*.

1906   Publishes first volume of *Das Erkenntnisproblem in der Philosophie und Wissenschaft der neueren Zeit (The Problem of Knowledge.)*

1908   Appointed *Privatdozentur* (lecturer) at the University of Berlin, after the intercession of Wilhelm Dilthey.

1910   *Substanzbegriff und Funktionsbegriff (Substance and Function)*.

1919   Professor of Philosophy, University of Hamburg.

1923   First volume of *Philosophie der symbolischen Formen (The Philosophy of Symbolic Forms)*; volumes 2 and 3 published in 1925 and 1929 respectively.

1930   Elected Rector of The University of Hamburg.

1933   After accession of Hitler, leaves Germany for England; Chichcle Lecturer at Oxford, 1933–1935.

1935   Professor of Philosophy at University of Goeteborg, Sweden.

1937   *Determinismus und Indeterminismus in der modernen Physik (Determinism and Indeterminism in Modern Physics)* published in Sweden.

1941   Arrives in United States as visiting professor at Yale University.

1944   Publishes *An Essay On Man*, written in English. Accepts appointment as visiting professor at Columbia University.

1945   April 13, Cassirer dies suddenly on the campus of Columbia University.

1946   *The Myth of the State* published posthumously.

CHAPTER 1

Introduction

I *Cassirer's Outlook*

IN an era when deep and long standing confusion has existed about the state of mankind, its future and possibilities, we miss the larger perspective. Ours has been an age of specialization, where fine minds address themselves to concrete though difficult and complex issues. We are the inheritors of a larger set of intellectual perpsectives left to us generations, even centuries, ago. These outlooks have long been internalized and the specific perspectives of society and man that today form the realms of knowledge have thereby flourished.

The dismay we feel at finding ourselves in an era of confusion, without strong philosophical guidelines to help us unravel the tangled contemporary strands, attests how far we have gone wrong sometime in the recent past. That our supreme generalists — our philosophers — must have failed us is an apparent and easy answer. Somehow, the tremendous dynamic of events has rendered rational decision making difficult. It has turned men away from thoughtful academic perspectives to a more involved and purportedly socially fruitful commitment to opportunity.

Ernst Cassirer was one of these generalists, a man whose life was committed to the larger vision of the philosophy of culture. He sought an understanding of the inner structure of knowledge in culture. Cassirer's general perspective in the theory of knowledge led not to the intellectual effacing of differences within the fabric of culture but in seeing the diversities and concrete realities order themselves rationally and logically in this palette of human activity.

One cannot attribute Cassirer's relative obscurity as a philosopher, as compared with Marx or Dewey or even Wittgenstein, to his attempt to understand the inner relationship between the forms of knowledge and the structure of culture, a highly abstract and academic enterprise. It was not necessarily because he was a generalist that he failed to catch the attention of the wider educated public. And although his scholarly approach differed from the more socially germane movements represented by the other philosophers, theirs was the more constructivist approach, committed to change, social or intellectual reform, heading in a direction in the movement of our world to which many could commit themselves. Each of these powerful personalities galvanized his followers along certain specific social or intellectual lines. Their abstract philosophical analyses were the key to certain specific practical decisions that could be made.

Cassirer's philosophical perspective rarely could be utilized in this manner. Perhaps the one great example that deviates from his search to *understand* and then presumably to allow others to draw the appropriate concrete conclusion is found in his last major work, *The Myth of the State.* Here, his analyses, both historical and structural, of the forms of mythical thinking moved him to warn us against being swamped by this form of thought as it overflowed its normal logical channels and inundated secular social and political decision-making patterns. It was as illuminating in the specific insights into our own situation at that historic moment as it was indicative of the larger impact and possibilities that this philosophy might have on our understanding of ourselves and our times. It now needed to be developed and followed up with as much immediacy as other competing and contemporary philosophical frames. Unfortunately, Cassirer died even before the final draft was completed.

If we can argue that a concrete realization for the lives of men has yet to be mined from Cassirer's philosophy of culture, we can also argue that for the most part the philosophies that took center stage during the first half of the twentieth century have also waned and lost their usefulness. In a sense, they promised much but failed us over the long haul. It is this concern for fertility over a long period of time that guided Cassirer in his conceptualization of the nature of philosophical enquiry and his continuing search for context.

It was the long view of the problem of knowledge and the structure of cultural thought that connected his views with a tradition that was alive in its renewed fertility. And it is this dialectic of enquiry within the Western tradition that was brought to fruition in Cassirer's writings. His philosophy has been of inestimable use in broadening our awareness of the research that has been done in a wide variety of disciplines that inquire into the inner structure of these disciplines, such as linguistics, comparative ethnology, biological theory, or the philosophy of the physical sciences.

Through Cassirer's philosophy we may be able to avoid these periodic renunciations of the past, the subsequent recantations, and admissions of impetuosity in prematurely throwing out the past. One of the themes that pervades Cassirer's corpus of writings is his injunction to understand the scholars of the past better than they were able to understand themselves, that is, to penetrate the inner meaning of a fabric of ideas of which the scholars themselves possessed only an inchoate awareness as they were forced to confront their own parochial intellectual problems.

Kant expressed this thought in his comment that we must understand Plato better than he understood himself. Hermann Cohen, Cassirer's teacher, gave this even more pointed emphasis in relation to the obscurity and complexity of Kant's writings. Ernst Cassirer, in interpreting the monumental historical as well as systematic studies of his forerunners, took special pains not to warp their beliefs in terms of any limited contemporary perspective. He tried to understand the problems of the past from the largest and most objective intellectual norms possible. In retaining our connection with the past, in realizing both achievements and errors, we can forewarn ourselves about being too quick to grab so-called certainties or dogmatisms. In this way, philosophy can allow the new to be absorbed into a structure of ideas that fertilizes the old, but does not overwhelm and efface it, leaving us intellectually naked, historically naive and arrogant.

II *Philosophical Task*

In focusing on Cassirer's achievements as a philosopher of culture as well as on the import of his work for our own time, we will note these several dimensions: (1) his antimetaphysical and conventionalistic views of the nature of scientific theory; (2) the philosophy of symbolic forms in which he attempts to delineate the relationship of the various forms of cultural knowing, placing science, language, myth, and art as equal and parallel manifestations of man's drive to see experience symbolically; (3) the more general theory of human nature, which he began to discuss and elaborate in Volume 3 of *The Philosophy of Symbolic Forms,* and which was more fully developed in his later *An Essay on Man.*

Interestingly, even as Cassirer's views are still concordant with the best available contemporary evaluations in the theory of knowledge and culture, they developed only gradually out of Cassirer's historical researches. All three basic aspects of Cassirer's theory of culture and knowledge, while developing from a fundamental approach to knowledge attained from his study of Kantian philosophy and post-Newtonian and Kantian science, were for long only implicit. They were only uncovered as he delved into wider and newer empirical domains of study.

What we have then, in addition to these fundamental approaches to great chunks of contemporary scholarship harmonized within a larger view of knowledge, culture, and human history, is a connection to the problems and solutions of the Kantian philosophical position and the more general Western post-Renaissance scientific tradition. Thus it is that despite a lack of contemporary bite concerned with the concrete existential dilemmas of man, Cassirer's philosophy provides a framework within which reformist philosophers might review their contact with the past and in so doing give historical substance and justification to our efforts in building a future.

Briefly, let us note and explain the dimensions of this philosophy of culture before we engage in a more extensive development of the origins and substance of his philosophical position. Our purpose here is first to hint at the fertility and compatibility of these ideas for today and as a rationale for the fuller development that will come in the successive chapters.

III   *Scientific Knowledge*

Since the time of Galileo, scientists have stood in awe of their method of thought and experiment. The scientific method has opened up great new realms of experience. It has pointed to events at far distant points in both space and time to predict what would occur and when.

As men of science began to reflect upon the new mathematical forms of knowledge that they used to explore physical experience, they inevitably saw this knowledge as constituting far more than a secular technique. With the expansion of each new development in scientific theory into new realms of experience, the philosophical desire to understand expanded accordingly. Scientific knowledge and "its" mathematical and physical symbolism began to be reified into an objective order that seemed to reveal the innerness of nature.

The epochal work of Immanuel Kant, coming almost half a century after Newton's death, can be seen as an attempt to integrate the specific content of Newtonian physics with an understanding of human knowledge and the reality pointed to by this objective science. In the generations following, as mechanics flourished, this vision of scientific reality dominated, if it did not overwhelm, all other existing visions of the universe. It was not until Einstein, and then quantum physics, that the full realization that Newtonian physics might be a special case of an even more general theory of physical experience caused scientists and philosophers to begin to pull back from their claims and institute a modest reexamination of the nature of science.

At this time, Cassirer, writing from within the neo-Kantian position, became a significant force in moving scientists back from their rhapsodic dreams of uncovering objective reality, toward a more modest role of filling in the gaps in our ultimate structure of knowledge. He showed quite clearly, through an internal analysis of scientific theorizing itself, in both the contemporary context as well as the historical, by referring to the old debates from the Renaissance through the eighteenth century, that discussions as to the nature of scientific knowledge were by and large tinged with metaphysical assumptions. How is it then that science, which evolves through such objective canons of prediction and experiment, could be infiltrated by metaphysics? Simply, Cassirer demonstrated, because too often discussions as to what constituted the scientific enterprise did not reflect the character of the actual work that went into it.

Cassirer's conclusions were clear. And they are as applicable today as they were in 1910, when he published his first important work in the philosophy of science, *Substance and Function*. Scientific theories are not reflections of a reality that is permanent, objective, and attainable in any one structure of knowledge. Theories are instruments of thought whereby the search to find order and unity in nature is fulfilled and through which further discoveries, equivalences, unities, and even diversities are uncovered. Scientific theories are fruitful if they lead the mind beyond the given concreteness of experience into a world of possibility.

The theories themselves, as conventions, are merely signs conjured up by the human mind as devices to make thought more efficient, to lead thought along its inevitable inner pathways. But we can never know beforehand what will result when we overthrow one set of physical theories with their various perceptual relationships and proceed to reconstruct these relationships within a system of signs that are worked into an entirely new organization of thought.

Science does not easily advance to new and wider realms of objectivity. It moves often by turning around upon itself, by overthrowing the basic conceptual assumptions of prior structures of knowledge and integrating the various regularities into wholly new patterns. It does seek to establish more universal relationships between things and events. Science searches for order, unity, predictability, but never from any preconceived theoretical standpoint of what the components of this unity will be nor their relationships within the structure. By looking back upon the various revolutions in science, we are amazed at the ability of creative scientists, against the all-seeing omnipotence of tradition and authority, to contradict the prejudices of the day, to reveal the implicit logical unity of heretofore unassimilable strands of theory.

An ironic element in the long, drawn-out search for an understanding of the nature of scientific theory is the realization that the laws of science are not written by an almighty God or by the obscure realities of the universe but are creative insights into the implicit unities of experience. For two centuries or more, we have succumbed to the mystique of science and its omnipotent offspring — industrial technology. With each new and awesome discovery, we have retreated from any critical response to its most apparent social consequences. The industrial artifacts, pollution, and social dislocations that have resulted from our inability to deal critically, and indeed skeptically, with scientific law and technological fallout are due to a great extent to our metaphysical intimidation in the face of these so-called laws of nature.

IV   *The Symbolic Forms*

The startling implications of this view of science, vindicated anew by his study of Einstein's relativity theory, set Cassirer on a new track, which, however, did not include the abandonment of continued study of the formal sciences. But it was now necessary to follow up on the meaning of scientific theory as an exemplification of man's creative and synthetic power. That science was a conventional activity that dealt theoretically with signs did not mean that it was purely idiosyncratic. Rather, the continuity of the main lines of theoretical and experimental endeavor and the interweaving of the various subsystems of scientific law implied a cohesiveness of structure.

The question that intrigued Cassirer and directed him in his studies was whether other cohesive structures of symbols existed. And if such diverse domains existed, what kind of inner structure of principles did they encompass and how might they be related to that most powerful symbolic structure, the area of mathematics and the physical sciences?

The Philosophy of Symbolic Forms, which was the product of Cassirer's first ten years at the University of Hamburg, especially in conjunction with its Warburg Library, an important collection of works in anthropology, religion, linguistics, and other social disciplines, represented this new line of inquiry. The three volumes, concerned respectively with language, myth and religion, and science and common sense, constitute a phenomenology of thought. Implicit in this line of research is Cassirer's assumption that no sharp separation exists between science and other representations of symbolic experience.

This commitment can fairly be traced back to his Kantian training and in a sense represents Cassirer's nod to the phenomenology of experience that is represented in the three critiques of the great Königsberg philosopher. Kant's first volume was concerned with the knowledge of physical science, the second with ethics, and the third with aesthetics and biology. Since Cassirer had already devoted much work to science, his third volume represents a culminating attempt to bring his earlier writings into harmony with the subject matter represented in the first two volumes of *The Philosophy of Symbolic Forms.*

A more interesting Kantian aspect of *The Philosophy of Symbolic Forms* is Cassirer's attempt to ferret out the inner dialectic of development that lies within each cultural form as well as the elements important for understanding the logical structure that holds each domain of symbolism together. Cassirer used three categories—space, time, and number—as a searchlight to illuminate language and/or mythological constructions.

He found that between these categories is an abstractive hierarchy in itself, that is, that space is more concrete than time and that number specificity and relationships are the most difficult, the last to be raised to a level of cognitive thought. They are useful categories in studying the evolution of scientific thought. And from the standpoint of their universality as logical categories Cassirer found them to be important structural elements uniting the diverse manifestations of symbolic expression.

But while it can be shown that for language as well as for myth and religion, the specific awareness of numerical relationships—beyond simple recognition of singularity as against plurality—is a later development culturally, intellectually, and for the young, developmentally, the mere fact that such abstract relationships do cross over the varied domains of human expression ought not necessarily lead us to dissolve conceptually one cultural form into the other. Each still retains its distinctiveness, even its logical autonomy.

The parallel evolution of these varied forms toward abstract and universal modes of thought should not cover up the reality of each distinctive and inner valence. Thus, while common sense linguistic activity seems to take its dynamic power from ordinary perceptual experience, its intent being secular and relating to the more prosaic activities of human life, there are other organizing principles.

In myth and religion, the realm of feeling and emotions, of empathy, fear and awe, love and hate, the sacred and the profane, infuses and alters the character of man's symbolic representation of space, time, and numbers. It is not merely that individuals are slow-witted about experience or confused with regard to causal relationships. Rather, man has an inherent propensity for, or a need to, create a mythicoreligious domain. Nevertheless, there is structure in myth and a seeming evolution toward more refined and intellectual abstractions of this inherent sense of sympathy. These are realized in the more nonimagistic envisagements of deity and the ethical development of religious doctrine and dogma.

Likewise, in the realm of the arts, the inner elements of sensuous immediacy seem to shape this symbolic form differently. And although we can envision highly refined art forms as being more abstract, cognitive, and even universal, it is impossible to experience or even symbolize the aesthetic universals outside their concrete exemplification. Thus it is that we can find great art not in a general and universal law, as in science, but only and always in concrete examples that come and go in history in a baffling variety of forms and media.

In this era of superficial scientism, it has been necessary to maintain a constant critical intellectual war against the kinds of reductionism that have seduced the educated mind in seeing art or religion in political or economic or even in scientistic terms and thus judging these various manifestations of man's symbolic acts in terms of alien logical criteria. It was to this practice that Cassirer was directly addressing himself. He wished to demonstrate the logical or formal as well as the cultural integrity of those domains of human activity. In his typical sensitivity to history as well as social context, he did not regard their existence as an aberration, a residue of the past, to be reformed, extinguished, or cast aside.

Each symbolic form needed to be viewed as a unique manifestation of human expression. Each had an inner logic that was the clue to understanding the perennial creative force that could be released within the form. And, perhaps most importantly, Cassirer argued that the application of the logic of one form of thought—for example, "mythological" categories—into the realm of secular political activity constituted a grave threat to the basic integration of culture. Great social and intellectual violations had been committed in the extension of religion to science. Ineffectual expressive traditions were fostered by the use of discursive logical patterns, such as in mathematics, in the creation of musical or artistic forms. It becomes necessary, Cassirer warned us, to look carefully beyond the surface of culture to the varying logics of thought that created both the diversities as well as the unities we experience. Only in this way can we plan to harmonize the richness and variety inherent in man and bring them creatively into the fabric of cultural life.

V *Man: Animal Symbolicum*

As early as 1929, in the third and final volume of *The Philosophy of Symbolic Forms,* there were intimations that Cassirer was extending the scope of his enquiry beyond the strict boundaries of the given cultural forms. Here, Cassirer attempted an integration of elements of the various symbolic forms—myth, language, and science—in a developmental perspective that also included an examination of childhood thinking as well as the pathological aberrations of the brain-injured aphasiac. Cassirer was attempting here not to efface the integrity of the symbolic forms but to face directly the issue of abstraction and representation that he had found to be an independent if parallel aspect of the forms. Thus we find in man his search for increasingly abstract and logical patterns of thought that seem to be forcing their way through the emotive, expressive, and perceptual character of experience in each domain.

Could this be a phenomenon at work that is representative of a more general feature of thought than is logically denoted in the particular structural patterns of, let us say, language or myth? Cassirer thus expanded his investigation into developmental psychology, even into the wards of the Frankfurt Neurological Institute, to understand patterns of thought that in the first case are largely potential and incomplete and in the second have been diverted from their normal course by the trauma of war-induced wounds.

These new empirical materials threw light on the historical, philosophical issues of the theory of knowledge. They also showed that the trend toward abstraction and the nonmaterial in culture, the progressive development of more universal patterns of symbolic expression in language, religion, and art was not merely a matter of sophistication and experience by peoples nor the purification immanent in logical patterns of symbolic expression. In fact, the theory of symbolic forms could not contain and integrate all these facets. Cassirer would have to adopt a broader viewpoint in order to elicit the full meaning of so rich and diverse a set of dynamics, yet with a seemingly common theme.

In *An Essay on Man,* written after Cassirer arrived in the United States, we see the most complete statement exemplifying the fruition of this line of thinking. Unfortunately, it was an incomplete statement, since there were questions that Cassirer himself raised that he was unable at that point to answer. The theme, however, was clear. These symbolic patterns of thought, the vectors that seemed to shape each form, pointed to a more generic problem. The dim outline of a theory of man was taking shape, and it was an outline that posed the question of human nature in quite different terms than did the more biologically and psychologically oriented schools in the English-speaking world.

Man, the symbolic animal, as Cassirer's more culturally oriented research indicated, was a creature of thought, meaning, and creativity. He was not merely a behaving, responding, adapting, and surviving creature. In this, man seemed to break the conceptual continuities in nature. As an animal along with so many others, man was a product of the evolutionary fires. The theory of universality demanded no sharp breaks or separate theoretical domains for man and the rest of nature. Thought could not retreat to safe sanctuaries of divine creation in order to understand man's uniqueness.

The modern scientist drawing on the intellectual imperative of nature's continuity therefore assumed that man's cultural products were derived from the basic adaptive necessities of the "survival of the fittest." Yet, as Cassirer interpreted the evidence, there was little in culture that denoted such clear-cut adaptive responsiveness. The search for symbolic envisagement seemed to indicate an intrinsic drive to shape experience into structures of cultural meaning more significant than simply baking bread, as the behaviorists seemed to indicate.

But this was thirty years ago at the height of a fashionable biological reductionism that infiltrated all the disciplines of man. Today, as we examine the far more sophisticated perception of the complexity of human institutions and cultural dynamics, Cassirer's view of man as a symbolic creation, *sui generis,* does not seem so farfetched. Our understanding of evolution is rich enough to allow for seeming discontinuities; our disillusionment with simplistic mechanisms also has sensitized us to the fact that man is a creature of inner depth.

If Cassirer was not able to spell out clearly all the implications for cultural theory of his view of man as *animal symbolicum*, he at least led us down a road from which our perspective of the past can point to a future rich in fertile questions. It is an intellectual road well worth traversing.

CHAPTER 2

The Neo-Kantian Tradition

I Kant (1724–1804)

M OST schools of neo-Kantian philosophy during the latter
part of the nineteenth century prided themselves on the fact
that they, in contrast to those which espoused the absolute idealism
of the Hegelians and their precursors, who also addressed themselves to certain Kantian problems, kept to the true spirit of Kant
rather than to the particular letter of his doctrines. This could certainly be said of the philosophy of Ernst Cassirer.

Although his philosophical studies ranged far and wide in terms
of subject matter, and certainly in his last years into the nexus of
contemporary social and political events, Cassirer remained a
staunch Kantian. He was in his own mind true to the ideals and the
perspective of the philosophical quest that Kant set himself. In this
sense also, Cassirer's philosophy connected, as had Kant's, with
the important intellectual issues that confronted the Western scientific tradition.

Kant himself was not especially historically minded. This fact
might have been due in part to his relative isolation in Königsberg,
then a small port city on the Baltic, an outgrowth of late medieval
trading among the Hanseatic League. However, he was a product
of that first generation of young intellectuals to grow up in the full
glow of the Newtonian revolution. Newton (born in 1642) had died
in 1727; he lived to be an octogenarian who saw his scientific work
taken up by the most brilliant minds of Europe.

Thus the validity of the Newtonian revolution was not in question, although its impact on religion was already being inquired into. Rather, it was how Newton's ideas could be absorbed into a
more general philosophical understanding of the nature of knowledge, how one could plumb the ultimate nature of reality and the

26

place of man in such an all-encompassing structure of ideas.

In his early intellectual development, Kant, besides pursuing the implications of Newton's cosmological views, had been immersed in the typical rationalistic metaphysical thinking of that period. Thus his view of the origins of scientific knowledge was that scientifically necessary knowledge came about through man's ability to attain to clear and distinct ideas that were independent of the circumstantial events of external experience. These *a priori* principles were somehow inherent in thought. In this way, thought and reality were joined in a widening and increasingly accurate mapping of the real. Science ostensibly was a product of the laying out of the structure of ideas; it was not dependent on the fragmentary character of sensations and experience.

David Hume's *Treatise of Human Nature* contained the philosophical arguments which, when they became available to Kant in translation in about 1772, shook him from his "dogmatic slumbers." Kant might have been generally prepared for these new ideas by the force of Rousseau's *Emile,* which reached him in Königsberg somewhat earlier and caused him to call Rousseau the Newton of the moral world.

Hume's analysis was directed at the rationalist claim that reality could be grasped without the intermediary means of sensory experience. In showing that this so-called necessary knowledge could not possibly be constructed without taking into account the process of perception itself, Hume relegated these *a priori* principles of knowledge to auxiliary psychological constructs, such as "constant conjunction," "imagination," etc.

But Kant did not accept this thesis uncritically. He did not feel that Hume had solved the mystery of the manner in which necessary scientific knowledge is established. What Hume had done was address a number of crucially important objections to the *a priori* claims for knowledge by the rationalists. The problem to Kant was now a constructive one — to avoid the extremes by which we "oscillate between a skepticism which doubts science because of the failure of metaphysics and a dogmatism which finds in the successful application of our *a priori* categories in science a justification for their application in a region where they cannot be applied successfully. The two ends can be permanently removed only by a 'critical' philosophy, which will show that the categories can be proved, but only for the kind of objects which we encounter in science and ordinary experience."[1]

Kant's systematic solution to this dilemma was the *Critique of Pure Reason,* one of the great monuments of philosophical thought, published in 1781 and reissued in a second edition six years later. It was a hurried piece of writing reflecting eleven years of concentrated study and almost twenty years of thought even preceding the stimulus of Hume. And it is in large part due to the opaque character of the writing that so many clashing interpretations of Kant have developed. More germane is the character of his solution, which was broad enough to lead thinkers along several different lines, especially in the light of the revolutionary events that were changing the face of society toward the end of the eighteenth century.

Hermann Cohen, Cassirer's teacher, thus echoes Kant's comment with regard to Plato. We must attempt to understand Kant better than he understood himself. No man can fully absorb all the diverse dimensions of a problem so large in scope in his own particular writings. And inevitably, as numerous commentators have shown, it is difficult to obtain a consistent and fair perspective on the Kantian position by a literal analysis or from a partial and non-contextual reading of his words.

What the neo-Kantians, especially of Cassirer's Marburg school, saw as Kant's preeminent achievement was the logical laying out of the formal elements that are involved in the production of knowledge. Thus, Kant refrained from concentrating on the fact of sensations or the categories of thought as metaphysical absolutes in creating scientific knowledge. He certainly emphasized the fact that knowledge is not to be seen as a passive creation determined by a given *a priori* structure of thought or imposed from without by an external world of phenomena.

Most important, the world outside, of real things, which he called "noumena," cannot be known through scientific knowledge. Nor can the inner world of the mind, the generator of the categories. Noumena may exist, but as far as the actual structure of knowledge is concerned, they are intellectual "limits," logically unrelated to the structure of what we know.

What the neo-Kantians saw in Kant was his concern with the formal structure of the element of knowledge — the perceptual manifold of space and time, the sources of our knowing, and the categories of our understanding that give structure to knowledge. The productive imagination schematizes this structure in a functional and useful manner, and scientific knowledge is thus generated for man. We do not search for an ultimate reality or a metaphysical substance either without or within. By the very conditions of the "knowledge situation," we are precluded from making these deductions, else we fall into unresolvable antinomies, or contradictions, of thought. This doctrine necessitates that we discipline ourselves intellectually and refrain from asking all the questions that we might. We must draw only those conclusions that are predicated on the basis of our formal analysis of the elements that are involved in the construction of scientific knowledge. We may dream of ultimate realities and substances, but these concepts do not clarify the relation of discernible factors in formal knowledge.

Even as Kant was attempting to establish the basis for consistent and necessary scientific principles in human experience, a counter and perhaps even more central theme lent perspective to his work in science and the critical philosophy. This was his concern for the moral factor in man. And even more central was the concern for establishing through a rational philosophical method the freedom of man in this nonmaterial domain. Thus, his *Critique of Practical Reason* has as its theme the concept of freedom, which in this case is not outside the limits of the law but is characterized by a self-legislating autonomy.

Implicit in the first critique is the idea that knowledge is a product of thought and that thought contributes a structure to experience. Scientific knowledge exemplifies the delineation of this immanent lawlike process inherent in man. So, too, in the moral realm, freedom, autonomy, and law are not irreconcilable. As Cassirer quotes Kant, "Thus the greatest problem for the human race and the greatest concrete task placed before it becomes the attainment of a universal law administering civil society; i.e., a society which is not founded on a mere relationship of might, a relationship of rulers and ruled, but which considers every one of its members as an end in himself, as a free agent who participates in the constitution and the administration of the whole and who to that extent heeds the laws only because he has given them to himself."[2]

Here we note what was later to become clear in the neo-Kantian view of the great Königsberger that the Copernican revolution in philosophy, by which man was to become the central actor in the production of knowledge, was a far grander enterprise than that to which even the Newtonian tradition would point. For Rousseau's concern with individual freedom and the relation of man to nature and society helped Kant to envision those larger perspectives of thought that gave a richness and depth to his perspective on man. And thus, in his *Critique of Judgment,* we find him engaged in an examination of the principles that underlie the aesthetic as well as the biological realm.

Throughout all these writings runs a common theme by which we can place the first critique's complexities and inconsistencies in perspective. Kant was in a sense creating a philosophical anthropology. In explaining both the limits and freedoms involved in the entire structure of reason, we can discern the fullness of man. But in so doing, we do not define and know man through one sweeping idea. Rather, our vision of what man is is constructed from what he does. And this only slowly becomes evident through an analysis of the principles of reasoning and behavior. These principles are diverse and can only be found by empirically and logically examining and describing the differing structural principles that underlie each domain of human experience.

II   *Early Neo-Kantians*

Perhaps it was the times that were changing. The Age of the Enlightenment seemed to disappear with the French Revolution. The disciplined, optimistic, and rational attitude toward human possibilities was succeeded by an era of turmoil, fast changing social events, and finally, a new romantic closeness to experience. In science, art, and literature, the forms of expression had tapped new emotional sources.

The careful separation of forms of thought, the search for the inner laws that determine the function of reason, that define the Kantian program evoked no great follow-up. If the words and external aspect of Kant's writings became part of the common philosophical discourse, it was a surface relationship. The great late eighteenth- and early nineteenth-century romantic idealists Schelling, Fichte, and then Hegel were not interested in defining the limits of philosophical inquiry into the ultimate nature of things.

The focal point of their attention to Kant was his concept of one thing in itself, *Ding an sich.* Kant made this a negative concept, in that as knowledge is concerned, we could never know the nature of the "object" in and of itself without its becoming "phenomenalized" in terms of the Newtonian space-time manifold and then being subject to the forms of the categories. But these latter factors all introduced experiential qualifications, so that we could never know a reality that was not subject to the structure of human experience.

The idealists were determined to search beyond. The progression went from Fichte and Jacobi to Schelling and Hegel. The former pair concerned themselves in the main with human freedom and the consequences of Kant's rescue of this dimension of man from the mechanists of the earlier era. The second *Critique* was a central focus of their writings and reinterpretations. Their hesitancy to place limits on man's freedom to will, to act, to think led inexorably to the views of Schelling and Hegel, in which the primacy of the mind was enunciated. Now conceived in a metaphysical perspective, the spiritual principle encompassed all of nature, man, history, and reason. The search was to grasp the nature of noumena. This metaphysical enterprise broke through the Kantian view that such concepts could only be "regulative" ideas and not part of the structure of knowledge. The absolute idealists saw the idea of spirit as a constituent dimension of reality as it really existed.

The delicate philosophical anthropology that Kant had erected to unite in one philosophical vision a truly humanistic perspective on man, nature, and knowledge, was shattered. Whereas in the Kantian enterprise the study of physical nature was to be but an aspect of the more general rational study of the principles that underlie the varying dimensions of human experience — both physical and aesthetic — the new romantic revolution sundered the two branches of knowledge. And thus, in the first half of the nineteenth century, academic philosophy came to be dominated by a metaphysical idealism of spirit while scientific research separated itself into institutes devoted to specialized and narrow theoretical and experimental work.

Perhaps the first real push towards the rediscovery of the importance of Kant came from Hermann von Helmholtz (1821–1894). Helmholtz, a man of prodigious interests and capacities, early saw Kant's significance for the development of a more philosophically oriented science. It was Helmholtz's wide-ranging interests that led him to search for more general intellectual roots to his experimental work. The outcome was a contribution to scientific thought that had important implications for physiological optics, mechanics, mathematics, and other areas of scientific research. It can fairly be said that Helmholtz helped put the physical sciences back on the road toward a great discussion of the philosophical roots of scientific knowledge.

It was Helmholtz's concentration on Kant's first *Critique* that directed the more general neo-Kantian attention to scientific knowledge. Helmholtz attacked the reigning absolutistic "copy" theories of scientific knowledge and argued that the sensations that constituted knowledge were merely signs of unknown objects interacting with our sensory organs. He also argued against Kant's use of Euclidean geometry as being *a priori* for all spatial intuitions. In general, he came close to a psychological interpretation of Kantianism in that he concluded that knowledge is a product of the impact of these signs of outside reality on the inner structure of the mind and that our ideas are formed and the laws of knowledge constructed out of a concordance with these innate forms.

Eduard Zeller (1814–1908), in a famous Heidelberg lecture in 1862, furthered the call for an analysis of science through Kantian philosophy by arguing against the holistic attempt of the Hegelians to encompass knowledge in one fell swoop. Zeller proposed instead that our conception of the nature of knowledge could only be built up gradually from a careful internal analysis of the structure of knowing.

A brilliant young scholar, Otto Liebmann, published a book, *Kant und die Epigonen* (1865), which seemed to coalesce the "back to Kant" movement.[3] In it, he launched directly into the issue of "the thing in itself," which had led the way into the metaphysics of the idealistic tradition. Liebmann argued that this concept was not an essential aspect of the Kantian doctrine and that, even if Kant had put it forward, it was a dogmatic residue that he could not at that time abandon. Whether or not one views Kant as putting forward *Ding an sich* as a "dogmatic residue" or, as Cassirer was wont to argue, as a "nonconcept," the way was now open to the neo-Kantian tradition to deal with science in a way that would discipline the materialism of the day in terms of a deeper cultural outlook than the antiscientific neo-Hegelian tradition of that day.

Almost simultaneously, in 1866, Friederich Albert Lange (1828–1875) published his massive three volume *History of Mate-*

rialism, which had exactly that task in mind. Whereas Liebmann's attack was on the metaphysical tradition of the philosophical idealists, Lange directed his guns at the covert metaphysical pretensions of the materialistic tradition that often protected its claims under the cloak of scientific objectivity. The world that we experience is a product of the interaction of sensation with the unknown. And while we know ourselves also only through this experience, Lange looked upon the laws of physiology and psychology as the only means for understanding what we are. Thus the material nature of the world is an interpretation based upon the phenomena of experience, and is ultimately understood by reference to the internal natural processes and laws that characterize our inner structure (physiology and psychology).

Outside our scientific world view, reflective of this inner biological structure, lies an inchoate domain of poetry, declared Lange: "Man needs to supplement reality [materialism] with an ideal world of his own creation," a world of value, "against which neither logic nor touch of hand nor sight of eye can prevail."[4] To the classical neo-Kantian of a generation later, this poetic fictionalism was repugnant. Cassirer felt that Lange's views represented in sum the ultimate consequence of any empiricopsychological interpretation of Kant.[5]

Lange, through his wide-ranging *History,* had brought fame to his university, Marburg, and made it one of the centers of neo-Kantian thought in Germany. Unfortunately, he died in 1875, at the age of forty-seven. But, fortunately for the institution and the philosophical tradition that had been here building, Lange in 1873 had been instrumental in approving the application of a young philosopher, Hermann Cohen, for a position as lecturer. Cohen had in 1871 published *Kant's Theorie der Erfahrung* (*Kant's Theory of Experience*), which had made a great impression. The treatise he submitted for his lectureship was a systematic enquiry into Kant's early philosophical writings. Upon the death of Lange two years later, Cohen was proposed by the faculty for the vacant chair and then appointed.

III   *Hermann Cohen (1842–1918)*

Hermann Cohen was appointed professor in the faculty of philosophy at Marburg University in 1875 when he was only thirty-four. In the next thirty-six years of his career, before retiring from his professorship, he was to make the name Marburg synonymous with neo-Kantianism. It was his goal to translate the great Königsberg philosopher's ideas into the context of modern physicomathematical knowledge. Further, his aim was to rescue Kant from the misinterpretations that obscured his transcendental method and thus to uncover "that Kant that nobody every knew."

Cohen was to become the teacher of Ernst Cassirer, and through his powerful personal as well as intellectual persuasiveness to remain the most significant influence in Cassirer's intellectual development. And while the mark on Cassirer was clear, it is not at all clear that the Hermann Cohen by whom Cassirer was inspired had the same doctrinal orientation as the student.

Cohen was born in Coswig Anhalt into a family of orthodox Jews.[6] At first, he was destined for the rabbinate and pursued these studies in the Jewish Theological Seminary at Breslau. His interest in this commitment waned, whereupon he transferred to the University of Breslau to study philosophy, especially the ancient tradition. In 1863, he won the prize of the philosophy faculty for an essay on Plato and Aristotle. These studies were continued first at Berlin and then at Halle, where he received his doctorate in 1865.

He returned to Berlin for further research and writing and apparently developed an interest in social psychology, for he published a number of studies in the next several years in this general area. But during this time, he also developed the deep interest in Kant that remained with him during his entire career. His first major essay on Kant appeared in a journal of social psychology and linguistics edited by Heymann Steinthal. In this essay, he joined the debate over Kant's *Transcendental Aesthetic* in which Kuno Fischer and Friedrich Adolph Trendelenburg (the latter a former teacher of Cohen) were engaged.

A year following, he published his first major work on Kant, *Kant's Theorie der Erfahrung,* amplifying his own views. And, as we have noted, his appiontment to a lectureship in Marburg in 1873 was followed by his appointment to Lange's chair in that institution upon the latter's death in 1875. It is ironic that this young Kantian, whom Lange had sponsored in Marburg, should develop an interpretation of Kant that would view the neo-Kantianism represented by Lange to be in gross error.

Cohen's willingness to overlook past quibbles with Trendelenburg and other critics of his views was characteristic. His search for truth was so intense, his temper and passion were so great that personalities, even his own self-interest as well as the interests of those around him, could not interfere. And thus, though there were active neo-Kantians in Göttingen (Leonard Nelson) and in Heidelberg (Wilhelm Windelband and Heinrich Rickert) during this last quarter of the nineteenth century and into the pre-World War I period, it was Hermann Cohen in Marburg who dominated the Kantian tradition. In Berlin, Kant's influence was evident in the sociological work of Wilhelm Dilthey and Georg Simmel. Indeed, it was Simmel who advised Cassirer to go to Marburg if he wanted to study Kantian philosophy in depth.

Cohen's logistic interpretation of Kantianism was based on his critique of the empirical, psychological views of Kant developed by Helmholtz and Lange. As Lange put it, "the whole of our experience is based upon our psychological organization; we cannot go beyond the circle, the limits of our sense experience are at the same time the limits of our human world." This view threatened the very universality and necessity that Kant saw as crucial to the establishment of the basis for scientific knowledge. After all, our psychological organization as we know it is an empirical construct and thus a contingent factuality. Here, too, would end Kant's claims for a synthetic *a priori* that would ground all experience in the laws of thought.

But there was more to this concern. In the original debate of Fischer and Trendelenburg, the status of the transcendental aesthetic and its relationship with the thing in itself were at issue. Cohen saw the logical structure of thought itself undermined by the weak grounds upon which the objectivity of space and time as *a priori* conditions of "possible" experience was established. As Hume himself had wondered, what establishes the principle of experience? And Kant could just point to the unknowability of "things in themselves." Thus a logical gap existed between "things in themselves" and the sources of the things as they became objectified in the *a priori* space-time manifold.

Cohen's solution was to reject the postulation in Kant of the passivity of the sensibility that depended in some unknown way for validation on an impenetrable structure of experience. Rather, the understanding, in its activity of form-giving, becomes the key to the building up of various forms of knowledge and in all functions

— feelings, perceptions, conceptions, volitions.

Cohen rejected any conception of thought or knowledge that predicated a state of passivity. All thought is active and we know its character in terms of its products. Thought is never psychologized in Cohen's philosophy. It is not the thought of individuals conceived of as a process. Rather, thought is the product of human efforts historically epitomized and completed in the natural sciences. And its validation in terms of its development and evolution takes place through its compatibility with the canons of scientific truth.

It is here that Cohen came to his own Kantian *a priorism,* even dogmatism, with regard to the paradigmatic nature of scientific thought. And it was with regard to his views as to what constitutes the core or model of scientific knowledge that Cohen saw his pupil Cassirer breaking away onto his own individual path. Cohen viewed as fundamental the differential calculus and the manner in which the possibility of motion is created through the intellectual process of integration.

One can find historical parallels to this view that the differential calculus as a logical process of thought stands as an intellectual source for the diversity of scientific factuality and the so-called real world of scientific knowledge that is thereby created. Thus, like Kant, who in rooting much of his *a priorism* in Newtonian space and time and in Aristotelian logic and who had already been shown to be in logical error by Helmholtz with regard to non-Euclidean geometries, Helmholtz eventually had his own Newtonianism displaced by Einstein's relativity. Cohen, too, left himself open to the same kind of criticism.

But, as Cassirer noted, Cohen was a neo-Kantian with strong platonic proclivities; he was also a purveyor of a rationalism that was tinged with Hegelian qualities. However, it should be reiterated that Cohen was not interested in the pure metaphysical spirituality of thought. His conception of thought was geared to the manifold creations that thought produced in the actual structures of knowledge evidenced in the various form-giving disciplines. Indeed, experience was the product of thought and knowledge its tangible results.

Again, mirroring Kant, Cohen also strove to go beyond science and to delve into the moral and legal dimensions of the form-giving power of thought. Going beyond Kant's more theoretical or abstract view of morality, Cohen tried to establish a concrete science, jurisprudence. Here, moral law finds its concrete embodiment in the concept of justice. Again, the concept of justice had to be more than a legal code; it had to be rooted in the moral imperative that established the autonomy of man from which the legal sanction of justice and the political power of the state derived its legitimacy.

In his later years, Cohen became, as Cassirer describes him, a mild socialist and supporter of the "underdog," the working class. Indeed, he found some sympathetic ties with the views of Karl Marx, without subscribing to the latter's "economic materialism."

During his working career in Marburg, he could not identify himself with orthodox Jewish beliefs, nor with the growing Zionist movement. However, his deep attachment to his religious heritage elicited his fighting energies, as, for example, against the historian Heinrich von Treitschke, who accused the Jews of being anti-nationalistic Germans. Cohen, calling attention to the ethical outlook of Kant and drawing a parallel between these views and the ethical principles of the Jewish prophets Isaiah and Jeremiah, took issue with the claim that the Jews could not be good Germans. As Germany is the nation of Kant, it must be the nation of the Jews as well, he argued.

The powerful advocacy represented in his writings and the force of his personality naturally elicited much latent opposition even within his own faculty. And thus, on retirement, he left Marburg to work in Berlin at the Institute for Jewish Studies, where he lectured and devoted his attention to religious questions. Here, he drew close to more traditional Judaic positions without ever abandoning his highly original reinterpretation of Kant.

His devoted student, Ernst Cassirer, found even in these later studies — to him somewhat foreign in their religious intensity — a significant element of religious understanding that would later be taken up in Cassirer's *The Philosophy of Symbolic Forms.* Cohen, while recognizing the origin of religion in myth, saw it as a great resource of thought that could eventually issue in the ethical and philosophical teaching of the prophets: "All civilization has gone out of mythical thought, knowledge as well as morality, poetry and all the arts. Civilization in all its different fundamental direction has unfolded from mythical elements."[7]

IV *Paul Natorp (1854–1924)*

One of the most important reasons that caused Cohen to leave

Marburg (in 1912) was the rejection by the faculty of his own choice for his chair in philosophy. Instead of appointing Cassirer to the position, they voted in a young psychologist. The one dissenting voter was Cohen's colleague and fellow neo-Kantian, Paul Natorp (1854–1924). Born in Düsseldorf, this second of the three great Marburg neo-Kantians was a man of extraordinarily wide and rich interests as well as accomplishments.[8] Inevitably, for a number of years in the shadow of his colleague and friend, Hermann Cohen, Natorp combined a deep interest in Plato and the Greeks with his basic Neo-Kantian systematic endeavors.

Natorp's systematic works are represented by *Einleitung in die Psychologie nach Kritischer Methode* (*Introduction to Psychology in Accordance with the Critical Method*) (1888), *Die logischen Grundlagen der exakten Wissenschaften* (*The Logical Foundations of the Mathematical Sciences*) (1910), and his most important theoretical work, *Allgemeine Psychologie nach Kritischen Methode* (*General Psychology in Accordance with the Critical Method*) (1912). In these writings, especially the last, we note an interesting contrast between Cohen and Natorp. Natorp's views can be seen as a corrective to the quasi-Hegelian tendency in Cohen's concern for a view of thought that attends little to the particularities of men and women engaged in intellectual activities. As Lewis White Beck points out, for Cohen, it was almost an accident that individuals knew anything.[9] To Cohen, knowledge of things rather than knowing things was of overriding importance.

Natorp's project was concentrating on the known, not as an object of knowledge, but as a source of consciousness. The subjective self is never known. It is a limiting concept, much as is the thing in itself. The true limits are held in a dynamic tension so that, by varying our attention from one dimension to the other, from the world of scientific law to the domain of conscious experience, we can obtain a fuller and clearer picture of the phenomenology of experience. Here, we would balance the varying dimensions of objectivity with the richness of the subjective. Cassirer quotes Natorp as follows:

But the inner world of consciousness can no longer be logically subordinated in any way to these three or four [objective structures of theoretical, ethical, aesthetic and religious knowledge] or set beside them or over them; to all of them, rather, to objectivizations of any kind and degree, it represents as it were a counteraction, a turning inward, the ultimate concentration of them all into the consciousness that experiences them. It is this ultimate concentration which the concepts of the psychical and of consciousness with its wholly concrete character must not merely ascertain as if it were something already given but which they must exhibit and in general develop.[10]

Natorp had plans to show how the unity of consciousness reflected the varying objective worlds of science, morality, art, and religion. In the traditional Kantian manner, he hoped to trace the structures of cultural experience by revealing their phenomenal principles. But here, Natorp would introduce a contrasting phenomenology of conscious experience in each of these domains. In this respect, it is easy to see Natorp's closeness to the schools of phenomenology that were then developing.

But there was more to this Marburger than this. Even in his student days, disillusionment with certain materialistic philosophical traditions had almost led him to undertake work in music. Writings in social and political philosophy as well as a number of books in educational philosophy reflect his interests and achievements. Toni Cassirer, reflecting on her husband's career, saw Natorp in the role of a perpetual searcher for truth.[11] He was apparently less inclined to hold to "system" than to explore. His anti-Hegelian search for the inner laws of the various forms of knowing and of subjective awareness saw knowledge evolving in infinite directions over an infinite period of time.

V *Conclusion*

From this perspective, one can see an inner tension within the entire neo-Kantian movement. First, the romantic idealists attempted to expropriate the basic terminology and structure of Kant's critical approach to knowledge for a direct explanation of the real. One can say that the idealists adhered to the letter but not the spirit of Kant.

Two generations later, after great advances in scientific knowledge, scientists with philosophical leanings themselves turned back to Kant to find guidance in understanding the meaning of the movement of scientific thought. This adherence to the spirit of the Kantian method necessitated the relegation of many of Kant's time-bound Newtonian and Aristotelian principles. The Marburg school especially attempted to cleanse Kantianism in the light of advancing knowledge and understanding.

Both Cohen and Natorp seemed to have followed their logical leanings in this attempt to purify the tradition. In Cohen's case, the conditionality of the human psyche pushed him into a panlogism, in which all thought in the production of objective knowledge was both synthetic — and thus creative — as well as *a priori*. And while he followed the particular directions of scientific knowledge, he fell into a repetition of the Kantian error in basing the synthetic *a priorism* on a particular form of mathematical thinking — the differential calculus.

In Natorp's case, the need to rescue the individual mind of man from this overpowering structure of objective knowledge pushed him closer to the phenomenological, where he sought for a breath of air from overpowering rationalism. Both scholars, in adhering too closely to the structure and logic of the Kantian corpus, may have thus allowed the movement to be brushed aside in the general rush toward positivistic scientism and existentialism; the alternatives seem to have been the antiseptic, aphilosophical adoption of the methods of existing science or the intellectual surcease represented by a more emotionally satisfying pursuit of psychological refuge in a world flying apart in social change.

Years later, when Cassirer looked back upon this movement, he would characterize it as a "gradual encirclement of the entire orbit of knowledge," an advance from the abstract to the concrete, "from the general principles of knowledge to the specific content of mental culture."[12] By the time Cassirer wrote this, he was deeply involved in his own phenomenological search for the inner principles within the variety of symbolic forms. And while he tried to remain true to an undogmatic spirit of the Kantian search for structure and principle in knowledge, it was probably true that the orientation inherent in his own view of knowledge would leave serious logical gaps. The question that Natorp himself had raised with regard to Cohen's relatively early *Kant's Theorie der Erfahrung* (second edition, 1885), that this system of critical idealism had uncertainties as to whether the sciences ought to be unified at the root or at the top, could be carried into a historically later stage of neo-Kantianism.

As we will point out, while Cassirer himself avoided his teachers' logical rigidity, the evolution of his philosophy nevertheless shows a sensitivity if not a solution to the need to account for a systematic tie between the symbolic forms of knowledge, in terms of the relation between man, the creator of knowledge and the form-giving structure of experience within which man lives.

CHAPTER 3

Science

I Cassirer's Intellectual Development

ERNST Cassirer was born on July 28, 1874, in Breslau (now Wroclaw, Poland), the first surviving son of an upper middle-class Jewish family. Although the family was large, Cassirer enjoyed all the educational advantages available at that time. It was not until late in his studies at the local *Gymnasium* (upper high school) that he showed unusual intellectual talents. It is said that upon his graduation, the faculty made special note of his academic achievements.

At age eighteen, Cassirer enrolled at the University of Berlin to study law. But since this was a choice made in response to parental wishes, his interest lagged. For two years, he wandered from Berlin to Leipzig, then to Heidelberg, and finally back to Berlin. In the meantime, he had developed an interest in philosophy. His search for a vocation was marked by an intense interest in a wide range of academic disciplines. Not only did he read voraciously all variety of scholarly materials, but he developed an interest in literary and musical culture. Germany at this point in its history was a perfect environment for a young intellectual who was intent on the breadth as well as the depth of things.

During this period, he attended several courses of Friedrich Paulsen, one of the leading German philosophers and one of many interpreters of the philosophy of Immanuel Kant. And while the studies were unsatisfying philosophically, they did stimulate his interest in finding an approach that fulfilled his own curiosity. In the summer of 1894, he enrolled in a course at the University of Berlin on the philosophy of Kant given by Georg Simmel. Then a young *Privat Dozent* (lecturer), Simmel was to go on to be one of the most brilliant theoretical sociologists of this century. He apparently provoked Cassirer's interest in the philosophy of Kant. And, when in discussing various problems of the great Königsberger, Simmel made reference to the writings of Hermann Cohen on Kant, Cassirer immediately obtained them. Simmel's discussions included the comment that though Cohen was the most profound scholar of the Kantian tradition, he himself was mystified by his views. This was enough to stimulate the twenty-year-old Cassirer to see whether he could rise to the challenge.

For about a year and a half, Cassirer busied himself in the study of Cohen's philosophical writings, and those of Kant, Descartes, and Leibniz, who figured large in the scientific orientation that characterized Cohen's Marburg Kantianism. In addition, Cassirer took on special work in modern physics and mathematics. A time of enormous ferment in the physical sciences, it was also a period of advance and of great intellectual controversy.

When he arrived in Marburg in the spring of 1896, he was prepared for Cohen and for the in-depth orientation of his intellectual program. During the approximately three years that he studied with Cohen in Marburg, Cassirer's interests in the historical antecedents of Kant increased. Perhaps it became clear to Cassirer, by now surely cognizant of the various forms of neo-Kantianism flourishing in Germany and the diverse philosophical interpretations of modern scientific research, that one had to go back and study these problems in the context of the larger intellectual and cultural issues of the time.

Or perhaps it was his particular slant of mind that made intellectual history so crucial an aspect of his work. Certainly the work of both Cohen and Paul Natorp strongly reinforced Cassirer's sensitivity to context and to the realization in an era of great ferment as well as advance that the blunderings of mankind in search of truth are not a characteristic merely of those who have inhabited the past.

Upon the occasion of his marriage in 1901 to Toni Bondi, a first cousin from Vienna, he received a gift of the complete works of Goethe. Bruno Cassirer, another cousin, who overwhelmed the couple with this treasured gift, was to be a lifelong friend. He was also his publisher. It is likely that he knew of Ernst Cassirer's deep love of Goethe's writings.

Hajo Holborn, a colleague of Cassirer at Yale, noted the similarity of Cassirer's historical instincts to Goethe's and indeed the similarity of their educational programs in mining the experiences and truths of the past so that they threw light on the problems of the present. Holborn quotes Goethe in this respect: "He who cannot account for 3,000 years is basically inexperienced and therefore can only exist from day to day."[1]

Very likely Cassirer felt himself unprepared for a frontal attack on the ongoing controversies that raged over the meaning of Kant's program, especially its status in an era of radical revisions of scientific orthodoxy. In addition, he was probably aware that an important aspect of the current debate hinged on the alterations that were being demanded of orthodox Newtonianism. And since much of the Kantian program in the first *Critique* was predicated on the objective reality of Newton's conception of absolute space and time as well as on the permanence of the principle of action at a distance as underlying the behavior of material bodies, it was well to hold off for the moment and look more carefully and deeply into the problem.

This decision meant a deeper historical understanding of the sources and controversies that led up to the Newtonian and Kantian syntheses. It was also clear that while Newton was well aware of, even though somewhat aloof from the controversies that swirled about the philosophical implications of his scientific work, Kant seems to have been more accepting of these problems. Newton's ideas had radiated into all sectors of the intellectual community in Europe and eroded the opposition.

This opposition was represented in the main in the writings of that powerful and all encompassing genius, Leibniz, at the time an enigmatic and to an extent a neglected thinker, especially with regard to the philosophical implications of his scientific and mathematical work. These writings, which were not systematically gathered together, became the focus of Cassirer's research. Yet Cassirer maintained the thread of a historical connectivity that necessitated delving into the writings of Descartes, at whose views Leibniz directed much analysis and criticism.

Although much of the research on Leibniz was completed, Cassirer, in 1899, decided to pause and present his research on Descartes as his doctoral thesis. Two years later, this one-hundred-page monograph functioned as the introduction to the more comprehensive and initial major philosophical publication, *Leibniz system in seinen wissenschaftlichen Grundlagen (Foundations of Leibniz' Philosophical Systems)*.[2] It is interesting to note that independently and just two years earlier Bertrand Russell, in *A Critical Exposition of the Philosophy of Leibniz,* had also seen in the scientific work of Leibniz similar importance for the modern world.

What intrigued Cassirer about the views of Leibniz was that in spite of his traditionally advertised metaphysical views, there was in him a sensitive awareness of the character of mathematics and physical experience. In contrast to Newton's belief in the absolute and external existence of an objective structure of space and time, Leibniz, the coinventor of the calculus, held to a symbolic view of knowledge. Space and time were forms of ideal experience, experience that is ordered by thought, Leibniz declared. "In order to have an idea of place and consequently space, it is sufficient to consider relations and the rules of their changes without needing to fancy any absolute reality out of the things whose situation we consider."[3]

Thus, space and time became relative truths developed out of an analysis of the logic of thought rather than from the inspection of physical reality. In resisting the views of space and time as mere empirical renderings both Newton and Leibniz nevertheless disagreed as to the ultimate source of their reality. As Cassirer later phrased it, "Newton is intent upon determining the substantial reality of space and time as two infinitely homogeneous things, independent of any sensible object. Leibniz no longer admits such a reality. According to him, if we wish to find the ultimate source of our ideas of 'pure space' and 'pure time' we shall have to inquire into the nature of our intellect rather than into the nature of things."[4]

Of course, Leibniz denigrated this symbolic knowledge, behind which he thought lay a more archetypal knowledge that resided in the mind of the divine intellect. Nevertheless, in the later nineteenth century, these symbolic views were already well accepted by many scientific thinkers. Helmholtz himself, upon learning of the work of Lobatchevski, Bolyai, and, finally, Rieman, had questioned the absolute status of Euclidean space in creating alternative geometries based on different constructions of the parallel lines postulate. And it would not be long before the Cartesian conception of the fullness of space and its ultimate reduction to geometrics would be seen as an anticipation of Einstein's general theory of relativity.

There was another aspect of Cassirer's interest in Leibniz that paralleled the general reawakened interest in this seminal genius, and that gathered itself into a series of systematic editings of his

writings, in Berlin, Paris, as well as Leipzig. Cassirer contributed
critical material to the latter editions. In spite of Leibniz's presumably Slavic lineage, in culture he was completely German, and it
was the consciousness of this heritage that stimulated an interest in
this first great Germanic enlightenment figure.

As with many German Jews of this era, given opportunity to
leave the medieval ghetto and participate freely in the expansion
and modernization of German society, the Cassirers had benefited
well from this nineteenth-century emancipation. And in contradis-
tinction to Hermann Cohen's intense and personal philo-Judaism,
Cassirer retained more tempered, if more universal, cultural ideals,
without renouncing his deeply felt Judaic heritage.[5] The Leibniz endeavor was in a manner a linkage in thought and feeling with those
universal characteristics of German culture that could easily become bridges not only to the Judaic intellectual tradition but to the
wider Western heritage. And indeed, Leibniz was himself as much a
man of Europe as he was a German philosopher.

Thus it was with some chagrin that as Cassirer contemplated
marriage, while agreeing to yield to Hermann Cohen's urging to
pursue an academic career, he now found it extremely difficult to
find such a position. Perhaps it was not merely Cassirer's Jewish
background but his identification with Hermann Cohen and the
Marburg school that hurt him. Cassirer pursued this vocational
aim, but without great enthusiasm; he had so much he wanted to
do, and the financial pressures did not exist.

He married in 1901 and that same year moved to Munich. His
book on Leibniz, with the Descartes doctoral thesis added as an introduction, was already in press; it was published the following
year. But he was engaged in a new and even more systematic enterprise in the theory of knowledge as it had developed in the context
of the great advances in modern knowledge since the Renaissance.
His intense involvement in this work was relieved only by his enjoy-
ment of the cultural life of Munich. Again, an aspect of his love of
the German cultural tradition was his deep commitment to its
literature, art, and music. But it was a critical or judicious love af-
fair, for there were even then elements in German culture that were
intolerant, nationalistic, even philistine. In this respect Cassirer's
widow later commented on their mutual dislike for the Wagnerian
wing of German music. But it was never an opposition that was
born of ignorance. They attended many performances of Wagner
in those days.

There was a momentary flurry in their Munich year when Tübingen University began negotiations to take Paul Natorp from Marburg. Cohen's letters to Cassirer were eager. Cohen wanted Cassirer to fill the impending vacancy. However, there was some uneasiness on the part of the Cassirers. Cohen's great synthetic work, *Die Logic der reinen Erkenntnis, (The Logic of Pure Reason)*, was published in 1902; and while Cassirer in the main still followed the basic lines of Cohen's teaching, he was interested in pursuing his own interests; he was not yet ready to make a commitment to any specific contemporary problems in the theory of knowledge until his own historical researches had brought him to the perspective at which he was aiming.

Being in Marburg with Cohen might extinguish this independent flicker before it had taken hold and revealed its own inner logic. Cohen's passionate friendship also embodied an intellectual embrace that could be overwhelming. Fortune had it that Natorp decided to remain in Marburg and this possibility dissolved.

The birth of a son and the desire to get back to the family environment in Berlin and the lure of the resources in the State Library brought Cassirer back to the capitol in 1903. Work on his *Erkenntnisproblem (The Problem of Knowledge)* continued; and, by 1904, the vast span from the Renaissance to Kant, with an introduction on the Greek philosophical approach, was essentially completed, to be published in two volumes in 1906 and 1907, with a total of over thirteen hundred pages. It was after the publication of the first volume that Cassirer yielded to Cohen's pleas to teach; he applied to the University of Berlin for the position of lecturer. But it was only through the help of the then emeritus Wilhelm Dilthey that he was awarded even this modest position.

II *Mechanics and Scientific Theory*

In the second volume of *Das Erkenntnisproblem* (1907), Cassirer makes an analysis of Kant's first *Critique* with an attempt to penetrate the essential core of the critical method in understanding scientific knowledge. Concerning Kant's method, Cassirer says: "Judgments about things rather than things are its theme. A problem of logic is posed, but this logical problem is exclusively related to and aimed at that peculiar and specific form of judgment by which we claim to know empirical objects."[6]

Having now completed a phase of his own independent study of Kant and the latter's relationship to the development of scientific knowledge up to that time, Cassirer was ready to pursue his own more synthetic study of scientific knowledge. And with the completion and publication of *Substanzbegriff Und Funktionbegriff* (*Substance and Function*) in 1910, he had made his mark in the neo-Kantian movement as well as in scientific philosophy.

The problems and approach represented in *Substance and Function* and in his various other writings on scientific knowledge are similar. As late as the *Philosophie Der Symbolischen Formen* (*The Philosophy of Symbolic Forms*), Volume 3 (1929), *Determinismus Und Indeterminismus In Der Modernen Physik* (*Determinism and Indeterminism in Modern Physics*) (1936), and the posthumously published fourth volume of *Das Erkenntnisproblem* written in 1940 and first published in an English translation as *The Problem of Knowledge* in 1950, the issues may vary, but the general theme and Cassirer's solutions remain clear and steadfast.

As Cassirer first faced the problem of scientific knowledge, a wholly new setting now confronted the philosopher as compared with the state of things in Kant's day. At that time, Newton still reigned and the connecting philosophical concerns were evident. In the hundred years since Kant's death, much had changed. Early in the nineteenth century, scientists were still exploiting the basic Newtonian laws of motion and optics for a variety of experimental areas and with great fruitfulness. But as the century moved to its midpoint, not only did fruitful theoretical work outside the limits of mechanics — such as the field theories of Oersted and Faraday — unhinge the absolute dominance of particle theories, but also the gradual transition to highly abstract conservation theories began to supersede the substantive views of heat, energy, and magnetism.

As great an intellectual as Helmholtz could develop a symbolic view of knowledge. At the same time Helmholtz saw Newton's laws as absolute, and all true knowledge as reducible to attractive and repellent forces. But, even if Helmholtz could conclude his study of the conservation of energy with the idea that it was reducible to mechanical principles on the basis of philosophical belief, other scientists were not so easily persuaded. And thus in the search for alternatives to replace the increasingly fuzzy contours of the Newtonian absolutes, various theories were conjured up: for example, energy and/or sensation as being fundamental substrata of knowledge.

Variously, waves or the ether were so viewed, and increasingly an agnosticism that either despaired or skeptically denied the possibility of knowledge was offered up to the scientific community.

Newtonianism fulfilled some of the basic intellectual needs. It was a view of objective experience that established clear-cut criteria as to what could be called scientific knowledge. The laws of motion, the action of attractive and repellent motions, seemed to demand of all material experience a conformity to these laws. The knowledge thereby obtained was objective; it described all objects in unequivocal mathematical and universal terms. In the most powerful historical claim of all time, it predicated that with every step of scientific advance, new domains of experience could be subsumed under these principles. Indeed, man could be said to be potentially in control of the inchoate diversity of experience in his contact with the objective reality of hard, massy objects. It was even claimed that the Newtonian laws themselves were our ultimate reality.

But as scientists pushed on in their investigations of natural phenomena, the new laws establishing functional relationships between phenomena were increasingly difficult to simply apply to the basic Newtonian model. A scientist such as Wilhelm Ostwald could now abandon matter in favor of a more fundamental substance — energy. Hans Christian Oersted and Michael Faraday, in their early studies of electromagnetism, saw the line of force forming within the field, thus seeming to contravene the Newtonian principle of action at a distance. Both Helmholtz and Max Planck, even though faced with a different kind of scientific law in the principle of the conservation of energy, could still hope that it was derivable from mechanics. According to Helmholtz, "Matter becomes the fundamental reality which has to be described in our scientific concepts of nature."[7] And if it cannot be directly perceived, Helmholtz averred in accommodation to his Kantian precepts, the validity and necessity of these conceptions follow from "the form of our understanding of nature."[8]

The wave theory of light, first put forth in the seventeenth century by the Dutch scientist Christian Huyghens, and the kinetic theory of heat were nonatomic theories and thus shunted aside in the strong tide of Newtonianism. By the mid-nineteenth century, wave and kinetic theories vied for scientific assent. Even James Clerk Maxwell, in the 1860s, following upon Faraday's work, was attempting to cloak his research on electromagnetism and light in the mathematics of mechanics. This Newtonian mathematical garb, within which no corpuscular entities could be found, puzzled many scientists. Which was the real, the symbolism or the wave phenomena that Maxwell was describing? Heinrich Hertz, one of the leading scientific researchers and theoreticians, advised his fellow scientists at least for the moment to avoid metaphysical explanations and attend to Maxwell's equations.

In this by now desperate search to find an intellectually stable reality and to find laws that would unequivocally describe this reality, another important philosophical alternative presented itself. Ernst Mach, taking up some tendencies in Helmholtz, urged that science once more leave the confusing if exhilarating heights of theoretical explanations of reality and return to the fundamental core of all knowledge—sensory experience.

If scientific theory reflects a reality, it is the basic experience of perception, says Mach: "The world consists of colors, sounds, temperatures, pressures, spaces, times, and so forth, which now we shall not call sensations, nor phenomena, because in either term an arbitrary one-sided theory is embodied, but simply 'elements.' The fixing of the flux of these elements, whether mediately or immediately, is the real object of physical research."[9] What science does is to bring the diverse but real multiplicity of things into economical structures of thought, thereby enabling us to anticipate experience and bring order to our world.

Nevertheless, even if we show that no physical theory reveals an external reality or contains within its structure an absolute value, Mach does not escape metaphysics. His view of the ultimate facticity of sensations — or phenomena — was a return to the old empiricism of Hume and the consequent metaphysical debates that swirled about the structure of knowledge. Like Hume, Mach found it difficult to show how the particularity of experience was transformed into the predictive generality of theory. As Ludwig Boltzmann and Max Planck noted, the ultimate facticity of sensations, their logical purity as compared with the conceptual complexity of the star, could not be supported.

It became clear that in attempting to find a solid starting point for scientific knowledge, one that would not be linked to potentially ephemeral and abstract constructs such as the atom, Mach had backed into another kind of realistic metaphysics, perhaps not a personalistic sensationalism such as that of Berkeley, but certainly a phenomenalistic realism that made theory construction a peculiar and almost *ad hoc* convenience of man. The usefulness of Mach's work continued to be in his sharp criticism of more sacrosanct theoretical absolutes in science rather than in their instrumental function for thought. In this light, his criticisms of Newton's use of force of mass raised enough questions to lead Einstein to his general theory of relativity (relativity of acceleration = gravitation).

Thus, by the end of the nineteenth century, leading theoretical scientists were quite hesitant to ascribe special metaphysical status to any particular set of scientific laws. And they were reluctant to identify some of the basic constitutive constructs: mass, atoms, waves, energy, etc., as the "reals" of the universe. Called into question was the objectivity, even the universality, of science.

The more scientists such as Heinrich Hertz, Henri Poincaré, Pierre Duhem, and Emile Meyerson pointed to the conventional status of the principles of science — how thought in its various manifestations created theory to serve function, mere convenience, economy, symbol — the greater the philosophical perplexity grew. Duhem saw some structure in the hierarchical and abstractive nature of mathematical physics. But it, too, only masked a Thomistic reality existing in the ultimate beyond.[10] Meyerson saw scientific thought leading to the extinction of the diversity of experience and to an inert identity of all substance.[11]

III   *Cassirer's View of Scientific Theory*

As Cassirer would point out in *Substance and Function,* it was possible to hold to a diversity of experience amid a unity of law. In the true Kantian sense, the structure of science will reveal itself not in the pursuit of ultimate reals, or in the heterogeneity of things, or in the unity of thought; rather, it will reveal itself in the logical analysis of the building up of scientific laws, in following its path from diversity to unity and back again, to reveal the functional relationships by which the variety of human experiences and experiments are tied together in principle. They are then utilized to stimulate the creative imagination to subject always wider ranges of experience to this logical structure of ideas.

The problem of the nature of scientific knowledge points back in the original Kantian sense not to the objects of science, a world out there, nor to a world within ourselves. Rather, it asks a question of logic: what kinds of theories, and then symbolism, do we expect to fit the criteria of judgments that we deem to be scientific? It is here that we find a common theme in all of Cassirer's scientific writings. If we study the rapid gyrations that scientific knowledge experiences during its moments of great progress, we will perceive a pattern in the succession of ideal models that scientists choose and then abandon. There is a pattern that even when it completes itself, as it did with Kant, must in successive periods of change be rediscovered. But, Cassirer believed, now that scientific knowledge had begun to be articulated as a methodological principle, it was well to establish its symbolic and conventional nature and thus forewarn future theoreticians of the traditional errors of metaphysics.

Perhaps the key to understanding Cassirer's view of scientific knowledge derives from his deviation from Hermann Cohen's views on the source of our judgments. The publication of *Substance and Function* came in 1910. Cohen had seen the proofs and had objected to certain of Cassirer's statements. The student deferred to the master for the sake of the unanimity of the Marburg school and made last-minute alterations. But even after publication, Cohen wrote to Cassirer out of concern for his basic logical foundation — of the "functional relation" in scientific theory.

To Cohen, it was an error to suppose that all laws were linked together by sets of mathematical equations that set diverse aspects of experience in functional relationships to each other, with no starting or ending point on which substantially to "hang" this logical order of relationships. Cohen argued that the concept of relation was a category and thus subject to something more fundamental. A category must also be a function, which Cohen saw growing out of the infinitesimal numbers. The infinitesimal numbers constitute the ground, a substantive, logical ground perhaps, but that which is the foundation of the entire mathematical and hence of the conceptual system of science.

But, as Cassirer was careful to note throughout his analysis in *Substance and Function* and elsewhere, this attempt to establish as an absolute any logical or substantial posit as the source, demands a principle of development by which other consequences, the very diversity of things become manifest. And Cohen's views did not resolve this problem. Whereas a strict relational view of science does not require logical or substantial origins or sources, it does allow us to traverse conceptually the structure of knowledge from particular functions to more abstract relations and back again. As Felix Kaufmann phrased it: The concept of relations "replaces fixed qualities by general rules which enable us to group 'uno actu' a total series of possible qualitative determinations. This is of decisive theoretical and practical import. As inquiry proceeds, thing-concepts are gradually replaced by relation-concepts, and a hierarchy of laws, stating invariant relations in terms of mathematical functions, occupies the place formerly held by a hierarchy of intrinsic qualities."[12]

Cassirer's concern about the status of scientific knowledge was with the question of the character of the principles that scientists claim to be scientific. They do not have a predetermined structure. Instead, they reflect certain logical tendencies as a product of the interaction of human thought and experience. These logical tendencies are such as to demonstrate persistently that substantive pictures of the world — reality as matter, energy, heat, or force — or even reductionist envisionments of phenomena — perception, neutral entities, sensations — are all limiting concepts in that they are end points of thought, whose undermining as sources of scientific principles can logically collapse an entire discipline.

On the other hand, the view of science as a search for functional relationships between diverse aspects of experience is merely an attempt to reflect the logical interconnectiveness of things. Logically, in science we do not try to find an ultimate substance or a phenomenal source. In science we attempt to postulate ever more universal functional relationships that encompass more experience within our intellectual compass. The physicist Max Planck realized this more general dimension of physical theory when he abandoned Newtonian mechanics as the basis for all conceptions of scientific knowledge:

If we look more closely we see that the old system of physics was not like a single picture, but rather a collection of pictures; there was a special picture for each class of natural phenomena. And these various pictures did not hang together; one of them could be removed without affecting the others. That will not be possible in the future physical picture of the world. No single feature will be able to be left aside as unessential; each is rather an indispensable element of the whole and as such has a definite meaning for observable nature; and, conversely, each observable physical phenomenon will and must find its corresponding place in the picture and finally the ultimate goal of scientific knowledge.... unity in respect of all features of the picture, unity in respect of all places and times, unity with regard to all investigators, all nations, all civilizations.[13]

This is an aspiration of science; it embodies a dream to incorporate all variety of experience into an intellectually coherent system through a step by step set of conceptual intermediaries from the most prosaic functional relationship to the most comprehensive and universal. Until this system is achieved, there will be sets of laws that lie outside each other, so to speak, each with its own ground and basic conceptual foundation — a concept of the conservation of mass, or the quantum, the speed of light, geometrical space-time. Each of these might be called an invariant of the system; they are logical *a prioris,* productive of a variety of principles derivable from their assumptions. But they are not prior to experience, and they can be challenged by experience. When they fall, it is not because of a final "experimentum crucis"; it is because the system of functional relationships must be so readjusted either in the light of new and wider integrations that the system shifts to a new invariant, or else the previous foundations are revitalized into a smoother interlocking structure of ideas.

The search leads always toward the universal ideal, to create means by which we can transform ourselves logically from one experiential domain to the other. But to do this, scientific laws must become amenable to such universal absorption. Science must renounce substances and phenomena for functional relationships that are purely ideal, logical, or mathematical. As one transforms material objects, pictures, or things into abstract functions, science can break out of the limits of the commonsense mode and more fully realize its own inner test of universality. One can thus say that the realization of the Kantian ideal — to search for the logical ground for all future scientific judgments — depends on the prevailing of two principles: (1) the universal subsumption of particular things to the most general and unitary principle, and (2) the progressive idealization of concrete sensory experience in favor of abstract mathematical or logical concepts as means toward which this unification can be achieved.

These principles demand no particular form for science. They are descriptions according to the most general consensus as to what will stand the test of being a scientific principle. In a way, they are regulative of the direction of scientific knowledge. Here we take one step beyond Kant's error in using Euclidean geometry, Newtonian space-time, or Aristotelian logical categories as *a priori* forms out of which specific scientific principles are constructed. It can be objected that the regulative view of science as seeking universality and idealization are much too broad and encompassing to stand the critical test of including or excluding any particular set of scientific theories. The reply must be that the scientific principles in their rich diversity in the past have been used to subvert each other. This practice has given rise to the expectation that the form and content of future sciences will eventually challenge any particular philosophical prescriptions as to what science should be like. Instead of setting scientific reality against philosophical identity, one must retreat to that common denominator that at least can help to direct the attention of the scientific mind to the soundest and most enduring intellectual perspective.

In terms of the subsequent evolution of scientific theory in relativity and quantum theory, Cassirer's modest proposals can be seen to have been vindicated. And in the process, the basic validity of the Marburg version of Kant's original insights into the theory of knowledge was upheld and deepened. In this respect, Cassirer's basic intellectual commitment to the fruitfulness of the historical perspective was likewise buttressed and enriched.

IV   *The Significance of Relativity*

Dimitry Gawronsky, one of Hermann Cohen's last students, a close personal friend of the Cassirers and a Kerenskyite revolutionary, noted an unusual facet of Cassirer's *Substance and Function.* Cassirer, who was so conscientious about keeping his ideas in touch with the latest writings, seemed to have ignored Einstein's relativity theory, even though it had appeared five years earlier and had received much critical analysis by 1910 (the publication date of *Substance and Function*).[14] Gawronsky used this curious omission to imply that Cassirer found aspects of Einstein's work fallacious, as he then launched into an intense, if theoretically wayward, attack on aspects of Einstein's special theory.

More likely Cassirer viewed this new physical theory as more than a mere addition to the problem of the structure of scientific knowledge. Cassirer's decision to hold off was wise. For, in the meantime, Einstein published his even more radical proposals, *The General Theory of Relativity*, whose postulates were buttressed in the 1919 astronomical examination of the "bending" of light as it passed through the gravitational field of the planet Mercury. Two years later (1921), Cassirer's monograph, *Zur Einsteinischen Relativitätstheorie* (*Einstein's Theory of Relativity*) was published.

The book represented an especially rewarding task, since it enabled him to argue for the philosophical usefulness of the Marburg approach to scientific knowledge as a productive instrumentality of thought. Cassirer's analysis of scientific theory as represented in *Substance and Function* helped to explain the successes and errors of the past; in addition, it could now help to unravel the perplexities of the present.

Perhaps the most glaring discrepancy between the Kantian tradition and Einstein's work was the commitment of Newton and Kant to a Euclidean mapping of space. It was clear that Einstein's integration of Riemannian geometry into his physical theory had to be faced. Kant had argued that the location of material objects and thus our objective knowledge of the physical world took place in an absolute space-time continuum that was Euclidean in structure. This synthetic *a priori* form of knowledge was fixed in the form of our perception of experience. Newtonian science thus reflected this basic perception of experience. But, as Felix Kaufman noted, Kant never argued that another set of geometric postulates would be illogical. The Euclidean postulate was not an analytic consequence of other postulates. Thus a different system would not be internally inconsistent with the logical character of "geometry." Kant's error was in seeing Euclidean geometry as a synthetic *a priori* necessitating the positioning of the objects of experience in space. This view derived, ultimately, from Kant's confidence in Newton.

But even in this commitment, Kant was ambivalent. In a variety of writings, he argued that space was not a real thing but an idea by which we organize our conception of the place and movement of things. "If I wish to imagine also a mathematical space free from all creatures as a receptacle of bodies, this would still not help me," Kant declared. "For by what should I distinguish the parts of the same and the different places, which are occupied by nothing corporeal?"[15] And again, "Absolute space is thus necessary not as a concept of a real object, but as an Idea, which should serve as a rule for considering all motions in it as merely relative, and all motion and rest must be reduced to the absolute space, if the phenomena of the same are to be made into a definite concept of experience that unifies phenomena."[16]

It is clear that Kant erred in his expectation that the Newtonian constructs would be coextensive with the theoretical evolution of physics. In his view space was a conceptual unity within which we order and relate the movement of objects in time. Space is not a physically real "thing"; it is a structure of relations. Thus, in terms of the general "critical idealist" position, Einstein's use of Riemannian geometry as a structural system by which new and more far-reaching empirical evidence is absorbed into scientific law and given interpretations that include previous principles by making them special cases of more universal sets of postulates, constitutes a renewed confirmation of this general philosophical ideal. The task of physical science, Cassirer argues, "consists in progressively relating the realms of 'forms' to the data of empirical observation and, conversely, the latter to the former. In this way, the sensuous manifold increasingly loses its 'contingent' anthropomorphic character and assumes the imprint of thought, the imprint of systematic unity of form. Indeed 'form,' just because it represents the active and shaping, the genuinely creative element, must not be conceived as rigid, but as living and moving."[17]

The same considerations apply to the transformation of Newtonian matter in the *Special Theory of Relativity*. Here, the idea of hard, massy particles having a real, corporeal substance is seen as a dependent variable. Matter is related to energy through a new set of equations, which describes the dynamics of bodies as they move through four-dimensional space-time in relation to a new invariant, the speed of light. As Einstein phrased it, "the inertial mass of a body is not a constant, but varies according to the change in the energy of the body. The inertial mass of a system of bodies can even be regarded as a measure of its energy."[18]

Now, it might seem that with matter not an independent thing moving in absolute space and time, the Kantian position would receive a further jolt. But if one looks beyond the specific Newtonian reals to the methodological conditions of Kantian substance, one sees a more "critical" element. Spatial and thing constancy was for Kant necessary in determining phenomena as objects. The category of substance provides the means by which sensory phenomena can be unified. Kant saw the logical necessity of fixing permanent relations out of the flow of experience. But this logical demand of his did not necessitate seeing this permanency as Newtonian matter undergoing motion. To quote Kant in one of his more critical moments: "... the representation of something permanent in existence is not identical with the permanent representation."[19] The special theory in no way argues with the fact that "something" is represented physically. All that it attempts to show us is that two disparate conceptual categories heretofore separated in theory can now be united under certain physical conditions. Indeed, matter and energy undergoing rapid inertial motion vary in their spatial as well as dynamic characteristics. The understanding of these transformations of seeming implacably opposed pictorial representations of experience — matter (hard and mass) and energy (field of force) — can be resolved by attention to the mathematical interpretation of their functional relationships, which extract from the vague pictorial images those scientifically useful parameters that become interchangeable factors in the evolution of physical theory. One can say that to the extent that matter, energy, space, and time are quantified in relation to the variety of interactions within the structure of science, they can be utilized as pivots around which the simplest "thing constancies" of scientific law gradually develop to the most universal and encompassing mathematical relationships in scientific experience.

It turns out that the total epistemological impact of both Einstein theories is a striking confirmation of the general Marburg critical-idealist position. The thingness, or independent substantiality, or reality of a variety of constructs is turned into a dependent function so that we can understand its import in dealing with the physical processes of experience. It does not stand by itself in any *a priori* sense.

Even the enigmatic nature of the gravitational constant that Newton noted, that is, the equivalence of gravitating and inertial masses so that attraction was always something external to the weight of a body, was transformed in principle by Einstein. Here, a real equivalence is noted between inertial motion of a body and its weight in a gravitational field. By integrating the situation from the standpoint of the different coordinate systems, where these measurements can be obtained, the interpretation will note the experimental factors as gravitational or inertial motion. What is significant is that this interpretation now takes place from the standpoint of different space-time coordinate systems. As Cassirer later put it, "All physical field phenomena are expressions of world metrics."[20]

By eliminating sensory and intuitive imagery, by going beyond the specific qualities of things, science opens itself up to unlimited possibilities — a structure of theoretical relationships envisaged through mathematics. The ghost of Pythagoras and the misty dreams of Galileo and Descartes, yearning for an all-encompassing understanding of experience through mathematics, are now reintroduced. No claim is made here about the nature of the world. Rather, our scientific judgments about experience seem thus to be fulfilled.

V *Quantum Theory and the Limits of Objectivity*

Years of study and contemplation of the import of Einstein's physical synthesis were fulfilled in Cassirer's insightful monograph on relativity. By the time the work was completed and published in 1921, new worlds had been opened up for him. Cohen was now dead, and Cassirer was freed of the fear of violating his old teacher's love by moving into completely new paths. In addition, a number of intriguing intellectual strands had been stimulated in his encounter with the Warburg Library soon after his appointment in 1919 as professor of philosophy in the newly formed Hamburg University.

On the final pages of his Einstein work is a discussion of the variety of symbolic times and spaces for each of the symbolic worlds of cultural experience of man. It is clear that Cassirer was already well into the expansion of his philosophical position beyond scientific knowledge into the other cultural areas. Yet his overall intent never was to abandon his quest for an understanding of the meaning of scientific knowledge, merely to place it in context. And for this he needed to pursue other realms of meaning. His *Philosophy of Symbolic Forms,* Volume 3 (1929), is an example of a return to the problem of the status of scientific knowledge, now in the context of other symbolic structures in the cultural disciplines. In *Das Erkenntnisproblem,* Volume 4 (1940), he again reviewed the achievements of physical science in the context of the biological and cultural disciplines.

It was in 1936, however, that his *Determinism and Indeterminism in Modern Physics* served to fill a missing link in Cassirer's philosophy of science, that of dealing with that enigmatic and controversial discipline — quantum physics. By contrast, there were few who argued about or against relativity after 1919 and the experimental confirmation of the action of gravity in altering the direction of a ray of light (as it came from the sun through the planet Mercury's gravitational field). In quantum theory, while Einstein himself was one of the first to confront theoretically some of the unusual experimental results, as in the photoelectric effect, the more experimental research proceeded, the more controversy obscured the meaning of these new principles. It was the philosophical implications of quantum physics that needed clarification. The limited experimental laws correlating the various concrete research yielded no disagreements; similar experiments always seemed to yield similar results.

What had begun with Max Planck's discovery of the elementary quantum of energy "h," wherein energy relationships within the atom or with photons of light always seemed to take place in simple multiples of "h," had been broadened year by year until an impressive array of experiments into the inner structure of the atom had taken place. The problematic results appeared to have given a dual nature to such elementary particles as an electron, either as a particle or as a wave.

But this duality was only an assigned description, for it was the particular character of the experiments that determined how one interpreted the result. The interpretation of the results had to be on the basis of a departure from the literal, unequivocal, experimental evidence. This was unlike the theoretically linked concrete transformation of matter and energy in relativity theory (atomic bomb) in that here the results were only statistically predictable. One could never predict singular events. Rather, patterns of waves could be detected given certain initial conditions; or patterns of scintillations on a screen, under differing circumstances, could also be predicted.

Thus, one could never determine both the "position" and the "momentum" of an electron. If the experimental arrangement is so structured as to determine spatial values, then one can predict the diffraction pattern that the scintillation on the screen can produce. If, on the other hand, one is concerned about the momentum, then the movement of the diaphragm through which the charged particles pass will give us precise results as to velocity. But we cannot so structure our experiments to reveal both kinds of information. In fact, the idea of the existence of particles or waves is unfulfilled. They are charged and diffused clouds of energy. But this energy is distributed in chunks or packets so as to yield particlelike results.

The basic constants of quantum theory, the various experimental correlations, have been fruitful in research into photoelectric spectra of elements, specific heat of solids, as well as an understanding of the inner structure of the atom. Given certain initial conditions, experimental arrangements, the theory predicts the consequences. But these results are probabilities. And compared with traditional Newtonian statistical mechanics or with Einstein's own work, the concept of probability is here of a different kind. As F.S.C. Northrop pointed out, the old manner of viewing probability is "restricted to the epistemological relation of the scientist in the verification of what he knows; it did not enter into the theoretical statement of what he knows."[21]

Thus, it was only a matter of observational techniques that led scientists to devise statistical methods for dealing with atoms. It was a mere convenience, because the inner dynamics of the system were known and could be predicted if one could observe the course of the interaction. In quantum theory, the probability relationships enter "theoretically and in principle; they do not refer merely to the operational and epistemological uncertainties and errors, arising from the finiteness of, and inaccuracies in, human behavior, that are common to any scientific theory and any experimentation whatsoever."[22]

A few distinguished scientists such as Niels Bohr and P.A.M. Dirac, among the great architects of quantum theory, were unconcerned by the philosophical "problems" that arose. Bohr rose to debate Einstein, who along with Schrödinger, Bohm, and DeBroglie, were troubled by the probabalistic structure of the theory. The latter felt that the theory could not stand alongside other foundational principles in nature because of its inability to give a complete description in terms of velocity or place of the particles and waves as they moved through space and time. The traditional demand that the elementary elements of external experience ought to be amenable to specifiable and individual determinations was here lost.[23]

A second group, represented by Northrop, Nernst, and Heisenberg, accepted the structure of the theory, but were gravely concerned by its deviation from classical statistical patterns. They saw this difference in the character of these uncertainty relationships to be reflective of a deeper mystery in the nature of external reality.[24]

With regard to the first objection, it was not alone the particular character of the laws that concerned these scientists. After all, the kinds of theoretical correlations of experience we could make depended as much on the amenability of the experimental conditions to fit into certain theoretical forms as it did upon the ingenuity of the scientists to devise theoretical symbols to reflect adequately concrete experience. One could continue to search into the empirical as well as the theoretical realm for more satisfying answers.

The concern was that the probabilistic form of predictability that satisfied the experimental conditions violated certain basic scientific principles. Simply speaking, one of the basic foundations of scientific truth, the principle of causality, seemed to be violated. What was especially exacerbating was that quantum theory diffused the clarity of certain key conceptual entities — mass, velocity, place — so that one could never predict the consequences of the movement of a singularly defined thing or event, even as one still could in relativity.

Cassirer's position was clear on this issue. It is one thing to be dissatisfied with the theoretical envisagement of certain empirical experiences. One tries to rearrange experiments to yield other consequences, and perhaps the theory will move in different directions that will eventually even out current dissatisfactions. It is another thing to say that because experimental circumstances cannot be symbolized in law with the same specificity as in other theoretical domains the new laws violate a principle of nature, and thus, in effect, consign the new science to an oblivion alongside phlogiston, the ether, or alchemy.

The causal principle, Cassirer argued, was not drawn from experience or nature. The ideal of law and order is a principle that we impose on experience. Causality thus

contains in its meaning the claim of "always and universally," which experience as such is never warranted in making. Instead of deriving a principle directly from experience, we use it as a criterion of experience. Principles constitute the fixed points of the compass that are required for successful orientation in the world of phenomena. They are not so much assertions about empirical facts as maxims by which we interpret these facts in order to bring them together into a complete and coherent whole.[25]

The search for law and order in experience does not require of theory a particular character. To the extent that the theory in one domain has the potentiality of linking itself to other domains, certain formal patterns will be more useful than others. But by itself, causality, as a demand of thought, required neither Galileo's, Newton's, Einstein's, nor Heisenberg's structures to fulfill man's need for a regularity of experience rooted in "idea."

With regard to the concern of Northrop and others with the "ontological mechanical causality" that probability played in quantum theory, another, perhaps simpler, explanation could be given. Since this interpretation of probability in quantum theory did not reflect a "theory of errors role," as probability did in the older sciences, the incomplete determinism, they thought, reflected an ontological character to reality itself. The inscrutability of physical reality might be relevant in helping us to understand freedom and indeterminacy in the behavior of human beings: ". . . potentiality and the weaker form of causality hold also for countless other characteristics of human beings, particularly for those cortical neural phenomena in man that are the epistemic correlates of directly introspected human ideas and purposes."[26]

Here, Cassirer felt, the symbolic representations of experimental conditions in one particular domain of science were being confused by being linked realistically with an unseen domain that was being described. Reality was not resisting man's descriptive attempts. One has to soar imaginatively far beyond the contextual circumstances of the experimental domain to think that the world could here only be incompletely known. A self-imposed methodological set of limits derived from the concrete experimental work in quantum theory was being transformed into pregnant ontological ascriptions. As Cassirer put it, the uncertainty relations "are not categorical statements about the objectively real, but rather modal statements about the empirically possible, about the physically observable. They accordingly do not presuppose a definite object only to determine subsequently that it will never be entirely accessible to our knowledge; rather they contain a new stipulation concerning objects which we may rightly use as long as we adhere strictly to the limits of the observable."[27]

We ought not impute to nature characteristics that are merely reflections of the character of our theories. Nature is not a given out there, whose mysteries are independent of the structure of our investigations. Thus, the loose ends of our theories should not be so construed as to be attributed to an inaccessible realm lying buried in the mysteries of reality or nature. Scientific knowledge is defined through our theoretical symbolism. What we know of nature will be created out of our theoretical investigation. Is it not somewhat arrogant to extrapolate from our temporary and local conceptions thus to characterize nature's knownness or inscrutability?

Quantum theory, just because of its revolutionary theoretical correlation of experimental results, jarred us, as no other theory could, into understanding what constitutes the basic parameters of scientific knowledge. It demonstrated the fact that as long as man searches for an understanding of the fragmented, diverse givenness of human experience, he will dredge up new and unassimilated materials having a potential for inclusion in knowledge. The materials of experience themselves will create the context by which thought will symbolically shape and order them.

Scientific law will thus surprise us in the new shapes that it will take. No reality lies out there to limit or determine the character of knowledge. "Reality" must remain a regulative idea, stimulating man's imagination, but contributing little to our understanding of the structure of knowledge. Our theories are free constructions of thought aiming to put experience into some logical ordering. When separate theories stand side by side illuminating the discrete domains that they speak to — the inner world of the atom (quantum theory), the outer world of universal metrics (general relativity theory) and matter energy in inertial motion (special theory of relativity) — there is a natural call for unification. This unification is desired not to efface the concreteness of experience but to order it logically. As long as the search continues to bring universal theoretical order out of the multitudinous character of experience, the postulates of our theories must become less concrete and visual, less like our intuitive envisionment of space, velocity, mass, acceleration; they will gradually shade into abstract functional relationships able to enter into new logical structures. Mathematical techniques gain in power as the two pivots of scientific theory — universality and ideality — become more central.

VI *The Power of Scientific Thought*

Thus, behind the metaphysical misinterpretation of the nature of scientific knowledge, a more modest picture began to take shape. It was modest only insofar as it retreated from the claims for absolute and permanent knowledge or claimed insights into the ultimate reals. In turn, this retreat from endowing various aspects of scientific experience, perception, or objective space-time, matter, or energy with ultimate ontological status necessitated a clear understanding of the purely instrumental character of knowledge, if indeed that was all that was to remain of the various historical claims.

Cassirer's work in the philosophy of science, insofar as it traced the concrete issues that arose from this revolutionary era of scientific change, stands as a powerful revelation of this new, more metaphysically modest, yet ultimately far more challenging, task of clarification and elucidation. For it was in the dynamic pattern of objectivization that the scientific mentality ultimately gave shape to the structure of scientific knowledge. Thought, in its scientific attitudes, moves from the stream of concrete experience to channel this experience into symbolically ordered regularities.

These regularities or principles are in turn absorbed into more general systems of principles, which bring a large domain of experience under their intellectual control. The principles of science serve to regulate and order what is known; they are also stimulants to look beyond the given of experience and to experiment with natural phenomena in a systematic manner. Then, inevitably, discontinuities occur, and experiment and prediction do not mesh. The search for new ordering principles and theories continues on a still more general level.

One might say that it is experience itself that becomes the pivot for new and comprehensive attempts to integrate the various principles of science. Thus, in the 1880s, the experiments by Michaelson and Morely with regard to the question whether the velocity of light is independent of the velocity of the observer (on earth) became a pivot for future scientific development. The answer as to whether we on earth were moving through the fixed ether was negative. Thereupon, the existence of the ether was called into question.

The conclusion followed that the velocity of light was independent of the velocity of either the source of light or the motion of the observer. The ether dropped out as a conceptual entity and the fact that it was now impossible to detect motion with respect to an absolute frame of reference — objective space — led inevitably to Einstein's revolutionary special theory of relativity. The experimentally ascertained speed of light became an invariant around which a great body of theory revolved.

In the same way, the experiments on black body radiation gradually led to the development of a structure of law involving the behavior of subatomic particles. But here, as the gradual experimental refinements took us deeper and deeper into the microcosm of the atom — to the very limit of perceptual experience — it was found that the character of objective research had to be redefined. The mere act of human perception into the experimental arrangements altered the state of the objects investigated. The demand for causal predication that inheres in scientific inquiry had to undergo a transformation. Instead of knowing the velocity and location of a particle with unequivocal precision, certain probabilistic principles dealing with the behavior of large numbers of particles and waves had to be substituted instead.

The meaning of the principle of regularity was not violated nor were the specific symbolic envisagements of law radically altered. The unique probabilistic shape of quantum theory was such as to reveal to us how much the demand for natural ordering and the unification of experience depends upon the concrete experimental clusters that are the raw grist of scientific knowledge. Nevertheless, it is apparent that the intellectual power of science arises from its ability to leap forward from experience to the more general, universal theoretical organization of experience. This is the direction that scientific knowledge and scientific objectivity take. But science is able to do so because it uses the symbolic tool of quantification.

VII   *Theory of Mathematics*

It is in mathematics, in the possibility of taking experience, of ordering it systematically and evenly, that experience reveals this capability for the universal. And, in a sense, the test for an understanding of scientific theory revolves around a parallel inquiry into the nature of mathematics. It is suggestive that at the time that the physical sciences were going through their upheavals, so too, mathematics was undergoing important investigations into its foundations.

In every one of Cassirer's studies into the philosophy of science, chapters were devoted to a critical analysis of this evolving dialogue as to the nature of the system of mathematical knowledge. The high point in his analysis of this contemporary controversy came in the third volume of *The Philosophy of Symbolic Forms,* published in

1929. Here, Cassirer attempted to integrate his views on the resolution of these debates with the general theories of symbolic knowledge to which this volume, "Phenomenology of Knowledge," is devoted.

There were three contending schools of mathematical thought during this period: (1) the logistic or realist school, represented by Gottlob Frege, Bertrand Russell, and A. N. Whitehead; (2) the intuitionists, L. E. J. Brouwer and Hermann Weyl; and finally (3) the formalists, of whom David Hilbert was preeminent.

The logicists can be epitomized in Russell's comment that logic is the youth of mathematics and that mathematics is the manhood of logic. Frege anticipated Russell's views of number by finding in number a rational status that was independent of things. According to this latter view, our knowledge of number was *a priori* in the sense that we "gazed" directly into the nature of numerical reality. But this rational insight is similar to that which gives us knowledge of the laws of logic.

And while Frege limited his attempt to derive the principles of arithmetic from logic, Russell (aided later by a collaboration with Whitehead) attempted to broaden this enterprise to show how all of mathematics would be related to logic in the same way as the theorems of geometry relate to its axioms. This was done by relating the concepts of logic and number by showing that number derived its meaning and objective validity by being recognized as a statement about a class. Such number concepts as zero, immediate successor, natural number, + , and × were defined logically, the natural numbers, 1, 2, 3, 4, etc., were defined in terms of their shared properties as members of a class or set of sets; for example, zero is defined as the set of all empty sets.

In the sense that mathematics partook of the vast rational possibilities of logic, this view of mathematics was realistic. It obtained validity or significance from its mirroring of this great structure of objective truth. Its growth and evolution would be mediated by both discovery and expansion of logical truths. In this sense, one could see that physical theory, in that it built its universalistic claims on the basis of the power of mathematical thought, itself participated in the uncovering of objective reality.

It was in part the similarity of the Frege-Russell position to the claims and problems of scholastic realism of the medieval era that made Cassirer hesitate. Also, a number of internal inconsistencies in this theory were brought out after the publication of the more systematic work of Russell and Whitehead, *Principia Mathematica.* One can summarize Cassirer's own skepticism by his analysis of the manner in which number theory was redefined in terms of logic. This he felt to be the essential weakness, for while certain logical relations seemed inherent in mathematics, one did not need to root them in other systems of thought (logic) in order to show their validity: "For in order to fill the class concept with a definite meaning, one must always invest it with the thought function of postulation, of identity and difference — the very same relations that are prerequisite to the constitution of the numerical concept and out of which the numerical concept can be derived directly, without detour through the class."[28]

Alongside this logical realist view of mathematics, the intuitionists, led by Brouwer, took a more idealistic and in some ways Kantian approach to mathematics. Intuitionism did not look outside mathematics for its source of truth and validity. Rather, in the process of the generation of mathematical entities by the mind, one could find both source and validity. The intuition of the whole number derives from the process of succession, iteration, ordering relations, and multiplicity. Number is an intuition, an intuition of pure process, of serial progression into the infinite. It does not take place as a process of counting in the physical temporal sense but rather as a process of logical progression, declared Brouwer: "This fundamental relation which connects one member of the numerical series with its immediate successor [n to n + 1] continues through the whole of the series and determines it in all its parts."[29]

In this view mathematics is built up on an internal awareness that there is always one more leading from the finite to the infinite. Along with this conceptualistic view of what mathematics is was built a constructivist aspect. According to Brouwer only those portions of mathematics could be accepted as being true that could be constructed through counting or calculating. George Cantor's argument that there are more real than natural numbers — and thus the whole theory of transfinite numbers — was rejected because it envisaged a task necessitating an infinite number of steps.[30]

Cassirer was naturally intrigued by the intuitionist position, especially as refined by Weyl in the interplay between his position and the formalism of David Hilbert. But, at this point, it is enough to note the weakness in the restriction that the constructionists placed on the development of mathematical concepts. Can the doctrine that numbers and sets be brought into conceptual reality even by a nontemporal and logical interpretation of the process of counting fulfill the task of mathematics? What impressed Cassirer was the fact that, here, mathematical symbolism was conceived as developing out of an essential tendency of the human intellect.[31] This was important, even if we sheared away the methodological restrictions it imposed on the nature and development of mathematical truths.

The synthetic attempt of Frege, Russell, and Whitehead to systematize mathematics, and the consequent paradoxes and weaknesses in the theory of sets set off energetic efforts to improve upon this logistic achievement. To the credit of these mathematical thinkers, the debates they set off helped to reveal the character of mathematics, the ultimate difficulties in assigning a "nature" to number theory, and the diverse aspects that mathematics contained within itself.

David Hilbert, the developer of what came to be called the formalistic thesis, phrased it as follows:

I find the objects of the theory of numbers in the signs themselves, whose form we can recognize universally and surely, independently of place and time and of the special conditions attending the production of the signs as well as of insignificant differences in their elaboration. Here lies the firm philosophical orientation which I regard as requisite to the grounding of pure mathematics, as to all scientific thinking, understanding, and communication. "In the beginning," we may say here, "was the *sign.*"[32]

Hilbert attempted to build a system of mathematical signs that were "concrete intuitive forms" having no external meaning or significance. The primitive symbols of the system were taken both from logic and arithmetic. Certainly the system of marks was given no logical meaning. We merely note the way the symbols or marks go together to make up the theorems of the system. This metamathematical analysis of the structure and consistencies of mathematics was to establish the internal consistency and completeness of mathematics without ever having to go beyond the internal resources of the system itself, as Russell and Frege had done. In the process of correcting the logicists, Hilbert utilized certain constructive methods of the intuitionists. In this way he was able to establish the internal consistencies of the proofs by restructuring the procedures.

Even early on, despite the power of Hilbert's model, there was opposition. Even if we grant the success of the formalistic, meta-mathematical method, Hilbert had turned mathematics into a monstrous tautology. What we now had was not objective knowledge, but a set of conventional rules much like those governing a game such as chess. For an intuitionist such as Hermann Weyl, mathematical symbols reflected an essential trend in human thought that leads it upward from the abstract givenness of thought into the concrete power of physical theory. For the formalist, theories are nothing more than signs on paper.[33]

Although Cassirer did not agree with the quasi-metaphysical tendencies in intuitionism, he also could not agree to Hilbert's purely conventional formalization of mathematics as representing its sole philosophical significance. Accepting the insights of Hilbert's method, one did not therefore exclude the placing of mathematics within a wider intellectual framework. But neither did Cassirer succumb to the formalistic aspirations for the completeness and consistency of mathematical systems.

Paraphrasing Leibniz, Cassirer argued that mathematics is a form of intellectual vision that rests on a primary and independent function of reason. Symbolic characters are only instruments of that reason. And in a key passage, which antedates Kurt Gödel's own more comprehensive critique, Cassirer said the following:

Even Hilbert's vastly broadened and deepened mathematical formalism never compels us, as far as I can see, to reverse this fundamental distinction. For Hilbert would not have been able to build up and enlarge his system of signs if he had not based it on the primordial concepts of order and sequence. Even when they are taken as mere signs, Hilbert's numbers are always positional signs: they are provided with a definite "index" which makes intelligible the mode of their sequence. Even if we regard the individual signs as nothing more than intuitively given, extralogical discrete objects, these objects in their totality never stand simply side by side as independent elements, but possess a determinate articulation.[34]

Two years after these words were published, in 1931, Kurt Gödel published his famous paper "On Formally Undecidable Propositions of "Principia Mathematica' and Related Systems." The conclusions of this paper were to show that consistent axiomatization of the natural numbers cannot capture all the truths about natural numbers as they might be embodied in theorems. Also, the consistency of a system such as *Principia Mathematica* or Hilbert's meta-mathematical program to establish the consistency of a mathematical system must employ metamathematical principles more complex than the principles of the system itself.[35]

With the ideals of completeness and consistency shown to be a hopeless demand made of metamathematical formalization, both the realism of Russell and the logical absolutism of Hilbert are compromised. As Barker notes with regard to the aim of *Principia Mathematica,* "If it were an independent reality of sets and numbers that mathematics describes, then one would have expected that the truth about that reality which would have to be consistent, should allow of being axiomatized completely. A reality the truth about which is necessarily incapable of being described in any complete manner seems a queer and suspect sort of reality — that is, not a reality at all."[36]

With regard to Hilbert's hopes for complete and consistent internal formalization of all mathematics, Cassirer seemed both impressed and skeptical of its ambitiousness: "... indeed it would scarcely be too much to assert that mathematics can only justify and preserve its old rank as an exact science if the task of its formalization, as understood by Hilbert, can really be carried to its end. For this would once again produce the logical miracle that is grounded in the very essence of the mathematical: the question of the infinite would be made accessible to finite resolution, to resolution through finite processes."[37]

Hilbert's search for complete systematization was on the same order as those researchers even then demanding of physical theories a specific form to their laws as a prerequisite to their being admitted into the domain of scientific truths. Thus, as we have noted with regard to his approach to the controversy over quantum physics, Cassirer later sided with those who felt the formal restrictions imposed by classical determinism exemplified the search for formal absolutes that could be rooted neither in nature nor in thought. In the same way, the intuitionists' demands of constructability were rejected as being unmathematically stringent. So too, Hilbert's aspirations, once deflated, necessitated that he retreat to viewing mathematics as a series of games, never to be completed, open-ended in consistency but signifying nothing beyond its symbolic structure.

There is a more serious defect in Hilbert's program. Even if we

grant its internal weaknesses, formalism was an indispensable instrument for establishing the logic of what has been already found
out, but it does not disclose the principle of mathematical discovery. It cannot explain the content of mathematics or justify it.[38]
In this sense, Cassirer reflected his support for the intuitionists'
constructivist tendencies.

In general, he was sympathetic with the aspirations of each of
these schools. Each had discovered a core of truth. The logicists
saw the deep similarity between purely logical thought and the
more specific and concrete operations and relationships of mathematics. Logic and mathematics do share such relational categories
as unity and otherness, identity and difference. But so too do these
categories find articulation in physical experience. And it is difficult to set priorities or attributions as to which derives from which.
To Cassirer, this would be a chimerical enterprise. Rather, these
disciplines share a more general affinity within the unity of
knowledge.

For the logicists, the close relational bond between mathematical
and logical thinking is reaffirmed. For the formalist, the purely
significatory status of mathematical systems is recognized, that
they speak only to each other in a grand, abstract structure. For the
intuitionists, their concern for creativity is acknowledged, even
though we hesitate over the restrictiveness of their model. Of the
three, Cassirer leaned toward the concern for creativity and
renewal:

Thus the work of mathematics never consists in a mere dissection, an
analytical unrolling of the already known, but in genuine discovery. Yet on
the other hand this discovery presents a peculiar methodological trait. The
road does not lead simply from determinate beginnings, established once
and for all, to ever more richly diversified conclusions: rather, each new
territory that we open up and conquer through these beginnings casts a
new light on the beginnings themselves. Here the progress of thought
always contains its own reversal: it is at the same time a return to its
foundations.[39]

It is the creative nature of mathematics that pushes it beyond the
current abstract structure, that prevents it, according to Cassirer,
from "freezing into an aggregate of mere analytic propositions and
degenerating into an empty tautology."[40] This creativity was nega-
tively reaffirmed in Gödel's theorem. In positive terms, the struc-

ture of mathematics as it points more abstractly toward logic on the one side and toward the physical sciences on the other reflects the more general character of symbolic thought. The fact that no structure of knowledge stands alone or receives its power for truth from some higher source must point, if indirectly, to the most pervasive relational principle. This can only be found in the symbolic character of all knowledge ultimately in the symbolizing act of man.

CHAPTER 4

The Philosophy of Symbolic Forms

I *Magnum Opus*

*T*HE *Philosophy of Symbolic Forms* was conceived toward the end of World War I but received its primary impetus only after Cassirer arrived in Hamburg in 1920. At the university, he found that the Warburg Library, which had been developed by Abbe Warburg and established at the University of Hamburg, had a perspective that paralleled his own. In fact, he noted to its director, Fritz Saxl, that it would be difficult to remain aloof from its attractions so that he could continue his own work and not be waylaid by the vast amount of ethnographic, comparative religion, and art materials, among other works in the cultural disciplines. As it was, he did utilize the library for much of the research that is reflected in *The Philosophy of Symbolic Forms.*

Toward the end of his monograph on Einstein's theory Cassirer had already written that the achievements in the theory of knowledge and in the exact sciences pointed beyond to wider significances in the scope and structure of knowledge. These achievements, whether one focused on logic, mathematics, or physical theory, seemed to effect a complementarity in that each discipline reinforced and lent depth of significance to the other. Each discipline pointed beyond itself to a larger structure of knowledge.

This fact inevitably led to a need to examine those less than exact manifestations of human thought, the cultural disciplines (*die giesteswissenschaftlichen Studien*). The great barrier or dichotomy that seemed to have developed between the so-called objective disciplines and the "softer" areas of knowledge could not be seen as a hard and fast separation. But, if no separation existed, then the problem that had to be resolved was that of the principle that connected the various expressions of man, a unity within which differences could be comprehended and accounted for.

The result of this search for a principle of unity in knowledge was Cassirer's major work, the three volumes of *The Philosophy of Symbolic Forms:* Volume 1, subtitled "Language" (1923), Volume 2, "Mythical Thinking" (1925), and Volume 3, "The Phenomenology of Knowledge" (1929). It is obvious from an examination of the scope of these three volumes that an enormous amount of study had gone into their contents. The intensity of Cassirer's concentration and the five years of immense preparation are reflected in the general difficulty in understanding this man experienced by even those close to him.

His father-in-law, Otto Bondi, stayed with the Cassirers in Hamburg for several months but suddenly decided to return home to Vienna. The concern, as expressed in Cassirer's subsequent letter to this highly cultured old gentleman, was that he not interpret Cassirer's lack of presence or his aloofness as a host as an absence of esteem. In fact, *Sprache and Mythos* (*Language and Myth*), published in 1925, was dedicated to Otto Bondi on the occasion of the latter's eightieth birthday. Cassirer's time was always deeply committed to his work. His lack of sociality was an inevitable result. This aspect of Cassirer's personality and the puzzlement of those around him were a sad dimension to the intense joys of scholarship and learning. But when one examines the scope of Cassirer's learning as reflected in his writings, it is easy to understand that such achievements were not built out of air.

The plan of *The Philosophy of Symbolic Forms* was not to search for an abstract structural principle that might serve as the pivot for a more general perspective on the theory of knowledge. As a good Marburg Kantian, he was skeptical of rarefied metaphysical constructs; he was determined to look deeply into the inner structure of each of the categories of experience that he had decided to study. Both language and mythical thought seemed to him fundamental. Both had been the subject of an enormous amount of intellectual inquiry in the preceding half century. Their study had evolved from the quasi-philosophical, speculative realm during the eighteenth and first half of the nineteenth century to the genuine systematic empirical studies given impetus by the scientific study of man exemplified in the work of Darwin.

It was the as yet unsatisfactory and incomplete theoretical digestion of this material that helped to motivate Cassirer. He felt that his Kantian perspectives, especially as they emanated from Kant's own early dream of creating a philosophical anthropology, was a natural entrée into this kind of research. The question that underlay his quest into the problem of cultural thought mainly concerned the *how* of the constructive experience. In a sense, it was a quest for the empirical piecing together of a theory that was internally consistent with our scientific knowledge of language as it is actually used by human beings, and with mythic, religious, and artistic patterns as they diversify symbolically in a variety of environments. Yet the logical structure must maintain its identity for the researcher just as mythic patterns, for example, are identifiable within the vast variety of geographical and historical locales where they may have been practiced.

The work of Russell and Whitehead had clarified and distinguished the particular formal structures of logic and mathematics and thus had established the basic principles upon which each could be considered a separate or related discipline. So, too, Cassirer felt than an internal analysis of each traditionally defined area of cultural experience would also begin to reveal its inner logic. In exposing the inner structure — the basic postulates and principles of elaboration — the inevitable relatedness of a discipline with other modalities of experience would be revealed.

The more general concept of a philosophy of symbolic forms was so created. The concept of symbolism is arrived at through the assumption that knowledge is a creation of man integrating the mysterious and ultimately unknowable data of human experience into coherent structures of meaning. Again, Cassirer is not creating a new view of knowledge here. He is extending what had by the early twentieth century, after the work of Russell, Hilbert, and Einstein, become axiomatic — that the exact disciplines of mathematics and science revealed no ultimate reality to man. These theoretical disciplines were conceptual directives for further research in the sense that their internal logic revealed an incompleteness of structure. But it was an incompleteness that was theoretical, a reality that lived on in the creative imagination. It was symbolic of meaning.

But in this conventional character of knowledge existed a multiplicity that tantalized. The separation of each discipline, its cooperative revelation of the richness of experience, held out an allure for the inquiring student. The inner structure of concepts in each discipline created its own particular aesthetic, though logical, valence. In other words, the uniqueness of symbolic logic, mathematics, and the physical sciences was derived from a distinct formal realm of ideas and experimental materials. And while each symbolic form seemed to be joined in an overarching structure, in this orchestration we call human knowing, the philosophy of symbolic forms allowed one to pursue the discipline in thought into its various branches and into new creative realizations.

Cassirer expressed the creative impact of symbolic thinking on culture as follows:

> Every authentic function of the human spirit has this decisive characteristic in common with cognition: it does not merely copy but rather embodies an original, formative power. It does not express passively the mere fact that something is present but contains an independent energy of the human spirit through which the simple presence of the phenomenon assumes a definite "meaning," a particular ideational content. This is as true of art as it is of cognition; it is as true of myth as of religion. All live in particular image-worlds, which do not merely reflect the empirccally given, but which rather produce it in accordance with an independent principle. Each of these functions creates its own symbolic forms which, if not similar to the intellectual symbols, enjoys equal rank as products of the human spirit. None of these forms can simply be reduced to, or derived from, the others; each of them designates a particular approach, in which and through which it constitutes its own aspect of "reality." They are not different modes in which an independent reality manifests itself to the human spirit but roads by which the spirit proceeds towards objectivization, i.e., its self-revelation. If we consider art and language, myth and cognition in this light, they present a common problem which opens up new access to a universal philosophy of the cultural sciences.[1]

It would be erroneous to believe that these discrete plans for research alone would fulfill the long-range ambitions inherent in Cassirer's neo-Kantianism. Hermann Cohen had died in 1918, just as Cassirer's perspective was broadening toward the conception of the symbolic forms. Paul Natorp died in 1924, when the second volume of *The Philosophy of Symbolic Forms* was virtually completed. It is difficult to say whether this latter event — Natorp was barely seventy at his death — forced Cassirer to veer toward a somewhat different task in the final volume of *The Philosophy of Symbolic Forms.*

As Charles Hendel points out, the third volume of *The Philosophy of Symbolic Forms,* which appeared in 1929, is probably

Cassirer's central work.[2] It is the work into which all prior writings flow. And it is the central core from which subsequent works take perspective and place. It is the achievement of a philosopher, fifty-five years of age, who has reached the peak of his synthetic powers. And in it, the historical, systematic, and it should be added, the empirical researches unite to bring the neo-Kantian tradition to a new level.

In this wide-ranging volume, the exact and cultural sciences are placed in relation to each other. The basic Kantian perspective on human knowledge gives them additional context and depth. More interesting is the fact that the primary hypothesis with which Cassirer entered into the task of *The Philosophy of Symbolic Forms* was now fulfilled. That is to say, by virtue of the empirical work he had done in conceiving this mountain of research — ethnological, anthropological, and psychological as well as traditionally historical and philosophical — he was now better able to see the extent and implications of the variety of symbolic forms of knowing. Thus, in his chapters on mathematics and the physical sciences, he was better able to articulate the significance of their inner structural character, and he was better able to see them in relation to each other and to the wider perspectives of symbolic thought.

But still, there is no transcendental position on knowledge. And this is perhaps why this volume is called phenomenology of knowledge. Here is an attempt to set forth a developmental and logical view as to how knowledge might be so structured and grow from its most inchoate expressive, affective, and mythical associations to the highly refined abstract symbols of science and mathematics. What Cassirer did instead of speculating on the possible historical and/or evolutionary and ontogenetic perspective was to set forth the logical and structural factors in each stage of thought. He was not yet clear as to the larger implications, even though his sections on developmental psychology and "aphasia" uncovered a new realm of study for an extension of the significance of symbolic form.

The dimension of phenomenology is not meant merely to note the fact that the book represents an attempt to see knowledge from the standpoint of its multifaceted expressions. It is, in addition, an attempt to lay to rest the remnants of Hume-like sensationalism and empiricism in philosophy and the various theoretical disciplines — psychology and physics — to counter and even incorporate the purely phenomenological tendencies in Paul Natorp's later writings and those of the latter's student, Nicolai Hartmann, as well as both Husserl and Heidegger.

If, before one sets forth the main structural dimensions of *The Philosophy of Symbolic Forms* a caveat must be interposed, it is with the relative incompleteness of Cassirer's own philosophical injunctions. For while *An Essay on Man* (1944) continues and extends the main theme of *The Philosophy of Symbolic Forms* and develops some of the biological, evolutionary, and cultural dimensions of the theory, it falls short of extending itself into a powerful substantive and methodological call to future philosophical research. True, the fifteen years that intervened between Volume 3 of *The Philosophy of Symbolic Forms* and *An Essay on Man* were years of great turmoil for the Cassirer family. Cassirer left Germany in 1933 — forced out of Hamburg by the Nazis — and embarked on a hegira that took him to England, Sweden, and finally the United States. This does not mean that his work came to a halt. Considering the circumstances, his creative output was amazing. Several major writings were produced before he came to America and completed his final books, *An Essay on Man* and *The Myth of the State.*

Cassirer's interests were perhaps too wide-ranging, his fascination with a rich variety of intellectual problems too intoxicating to be restrained. The significance of his vision of man and knowledge in terms of the symbolic form principle was apparent. He came to understand its perplexity and its "pregnance." But as it was gradually distilled during a time of turmoil, he could not be expected to pivot from one set of philosophical issues and contexts and immerse himself in those rich empirical realms that the evolutioary, moral, and historical implications of his ideas seemed to call for. Most appropriate to his Kantianism, perhaps, was the fact that the phenomena we call knowledge and the *animal symbolicum* we call man were yet to be revealed completely.

II *Language*

The special challenge that the study of language presents from the standpoint of the philosophy of culture is that language is both a content and a vehicle. It is a given content because all peoples use it on a mundane intuitive and functional level. As such, it reflects the specialized use that is reflected in the most broad-ranged activities of a society as a whole. It is a vehicle because through language many specialized psychological uses can be given form. With language, we can not only speak to the plumber and the greengrocer, but also whisper love poetry or discuss the abstract issues of value theory with scholars. The distance between the streets of the urban ghetto and the mountaintop observatory of a university research team may only be a few miles. But the levels of the linguistic discourse are perhaps millennia apart.

The significance of these facts had long preoccupied scholars. By the time of Cassirer's research, the original Indo-European bias of linguistic scholars had been tempered by a more universal ethnographic awareness of the distinction in language between structure and content. It was this fact, that a variety of grammatical structures showing no inherent superiority should issue into such diverse cultural attainments, that intrigued Cassirer.

In keeping with his scholarly sensitivity and his cherishing of the cultural values of civilized life, Cassirer maintained that language needed to be understood at least as much for its civilizing adaptiveness and its cultural potentiality in the arts, sciences, and philosophy as it could be understood in terms of its functional neutrality. Even if the structure of syntax and grammar gave us no internal clue to the state of culture, certainly the fact that some peoples had attained a higher level of civilization must be reflective of more than a linguistic accident.

Much contemporary literature concerns the relationship of thought and language. Cassirer did not confront this issue directly, since the problem then was not couched in specific conceptual terms as it has been recently in physiological and developmental psychology. But he did recognize that the difference in function between the naive native and the mathematical theorist had to reflect a development of thought that represented more than a mere restructuring of language itself. As a matter of fact, he was drawn, in Volume 3 of *The Philosophy of Symbolic Forms,* to the developmental problem in order to answer to the historical and cultural one:

In the development of the child there is no doubt that the intuition of the world of things does not exist from the beginning but must in a sense be wrested from the world of language. The first "names" which the child masters and uses with understanding seem to designate no fixed and permanent objects, but only more or less fluid and vague general impressions. Any change in these general impressions, however slight from our standpoint, suffices to prevent the use of the same name.... Only as the word is freed from the initial restriction, only when it is apprehended in its universal signification and applicability, does the new horizon of the "thing" arise in the child's consciousness. Here again it is the awakening of the symbolic consciousness as such which seems to open this new horizon. All observers agree in describing the almost insatiable hunger for names which seizes the child at this point; he wants to know the name of every new impression.... It is no empty mental game but an original urge toward objective intuition. The hunger for names is ultimately a hunger for forms, an urge for essential apprehension.[3]

Thus we have Cassirer's fundamental position. The search for structure is inherent in thought. But language, which is a vehicle of expression peculiar to man, becomes caught up in the inner trend. Ultimately, language itself becomes the container, the basic form by which man's search for symbolic coherence is established. One can see language as the practical exemplification of the purely philosophical debate between the Kantians and Humeans. The emptiness and passivity that are exemplified in theoretical empiricism are given tangible significance when one turns to language.

We know linguistically as we know experientially. Sounds, like sensations, do not impress themselves into our minds as bare essences. They carry no raw intellectual significance. Rather, they are vehicles or means by which the form-giving powers of thought gradually shape sound into meanings. The child's world, the denotations of which flow into and out of objects with each momentary change of state, and in turn the circumstances of his intellectual and experiential development, is only gradually divided into logical categories that allow him to stabilize experience. Finally, through the language of his group, a coherent world of things, people, and ideas is ordered that suffices for his needs.

But it is not enough for Cassirer's theory of language to show that each individual comes to an intuitive symbolic use of his vocal chords and his auditory facility to use and respond to speech in terms of the abstract system of meaning that is language. This is surely a creative miracle which when compared with animal signals loomed larger and larger in Cassirer's view of the problem as the years wore on. At this early point in his study of cultural thought, what needed to be accounted for as much as the creative symbolic act that is embedded in the idea of a "name" was the historical process seen as a logical pattern of development that leads language along the road of intellectual development. Then must come the building up of civilization and high culture.

The theme that ranked high with Cassirer was originally developed by H. Usener in 1896. Writing on the concept of "divine names," *Götternamen,* Usener was interested in finding the inner principles that seemed to lie immanent in the evolution of mythical ideas. In *Language and Myth,* Cassirer quoted Usener approvingly:

> There have been long periods in mental evolution when the human mind was slowly laboring toward thought and conception and was following quite different laws of ideation and speech.... The chasm between specific perception and general concepts is far greater than our academic notions, and a language which does our thinking for us, lead us to suppose. It is so great that I cannot imagine how it could have been bridged, had not language itself without man's conscious awareness, prepared and induced the process. It is language that causes the multitude of casual, individual expressions to yield up "one" which extends its denotation over more and more special cases, until it comes to denote them all, and assumes the power of expressing a class concept.[4]

Here is a hint of linguistic realism in the implication that language itself is the propelling force leading outward toward the less particular, personal, emotional, and toward abstraction and generalization. Cassirer hedged; for in this realism are elements of what has since come to imply a Whorfeian view of language, that is, that language itself, its form and content, shapes the mind. Cassirer says at a later point in *Language and Myth:*

> Should we not suppose, for instance, that the way which inflected languages have of endowing every noun with a particular gender may have influenced the conceptions of mythico-religious imagination and bent them after its own fashion? Or may we deem it mere chance that among peoples whose language does not differentiate genders, but employs other and more complex principles of classification, the realm of myth and religion also exhibits an entirely different structure — that it represents all phases of existence not under the auspices of personal, divine powers, but orders it according to totemic groups and classes?[5]

He left it to science to enquire further into the issue. It is enough to say that language as form and the varied psychological contents of myth, religion, or art do act on each other to shape the character and destiny of culture. The contents upon which language thus acts, whether intuitive linguistic experience or myth or art, are varied. And, though they are obviously the products of a unified structure of thought in the individual, we can never clearly identify that innerness which language reflects. Kantian philosophers have called it "spiritual." Rather, this innerness of mind is an intellectual or logical limit that is revealed by its various products. In essence, the human mind, which to an extent leads language along its own particular road of development, is a functional construct that is never known purely in and for itself. It is a limit, a noumenon, which we can know only by its activity.

Cassirer was well aware that the research in the various disciplines, in spite of conscious attempts to limit parochial historical and conceptual preconceptions, was suffused with the Western approach to experience. Yet, he was also conscious of the manner in which twentieth-century science and philosophy had extended themselves to encompass the expanding arc of Western cultural domination. Thus, there existed a latent universalism in the method of analysis that Cassirer adopted in *The Philosophy of Symbolic Forms*.

Simply, he used three measures by which one could conceptualize the relative evolution of the various symbolic forms. Space, time, and number he felt to be basic experiential categories of all people. In dealing with conventional social experience — language, myth, religion, and art — these Newtonian-Kantian categories were utilized to clarify the ordering of the experienced. One ought not be so naive as to think that Cassirer delved into the historic and comparative materials with no sense of what he was looking for or what he would find. But, on the other hand, it would be unfair to him to argue that he could foresee the full measure of understanding or the shape of the results that such a conceptual framework would reveal.

The concepts of space, time, and number are not given to man in one fell swoop. They are in a sense immanent in thought and in culture. For, after all, it is the same human mind that first expresses his sense of space through the metaphor of his body: back—behind, neck—on, belly—in, eye—in front of, etc.[6] How much refinement of thought and experience and merely time on this earth does it take for a people to advance to the abstract mathematical view of space as given by Descartes or Einstein?

At first, language reflects this sensuosity of experience. Space is first noted and expressed in terms of concrete and personal categories. The body acts as a guide or reference point to note the variety of spatial relations that have to be coordinated linguistically as well as intellectually. And, even as these words begin to be abstracted in reference to more general spatial categories, the words remain as metaphorical reminders of their original purposes.

Thus, as the relatively fixed sense of space that is extrapolated from one's own body is extended to a sense of action or activity, the dynamic sense of life is given familiarity and structure by its association with personal linguistic images. Thus, activities usually take place within spatial contexts: "He is working in the field" is transformed linguistically into "...inside the field." Children playing on the street becomes "...on the surface of the street." A dynamic activity outside one's own periphery becomes related to pronouns expressing the second and third person. Thus, I, thou, and he are linguistically related to *hier, da,* and *dort.*

Helmholtz was probably the first to note how personal relationships in terms of decreasing familiarity are related to spatial categories in a wide variety of languages. The Cherokees, for example, have nine third-person pronouns to characterize certain activities. Australian languages express the idea that a man has struck a dog with a spear as "'up front' has stuck the dog 'back there' with this or that weapon."[7]

Time is a more abstract conception. And, as would be expected, the linguistic expression of time seems to be more inchoately reflected in language as compared with space. Thus, as with the development of child language, the sense of now and not now is an early intuition. It is similar to the spatial here and there. But where spatial distinctions using one's own body or the relative distances of other personal relations become fairly succinct in pointing to subtle spatial gradations, time usually remains indistinctly categorized. Even the numerous intuitively constructed grammatical "tenses" of some primitive languages are usually qualitative and modal distinctions of "earlier" and "later" and not strictly past and future.[8] In some simple societies, expression of time "makes distinction as to whether an action begins 'suddenly' or develops gradually, whether it is abrupt or continuous, whether it constitutes a single undivided whole or takes place in similar, rhythmically recurrent phases. But for the concrete orientation which language still retains, these differences are not so much conceptual as intuitive, not so much quantitative as qualitative ... every single event expressed by a specific mood has, one might say, a 'time of its own.'"[9]

The concept of number represents the problem and the paradox of the relationship between thought and language. For while space and time can be gradually distilled and refined to a high degree linguistically, the idea of number is impoverished to the extent that it is immersed in the natural language. It must free itself symbolically in order to express fully the intellectual power inherent in its possibilities. Cassirer sees the use of number as a verbal sign as an inevitable first step. But, while the verbal expression of number is an important dialectical stage in the evolution of the concept, language inevitably creates a tension, an "opposition" that prevents number from fulfilling its potentiality. Language is rooted in the intuitive mode, in the concrete world of objects and processes, in sensory things and in particularities. Yet, somehow, Cassirer noted:

> The dialectical principle of progress is confirmed: the more language, in the course of its development, seems to immerse itself in the expression of sensuous things, the more effectively it contributes to the spiritual process of liberation from the sensuous. It is through material enumerable things, however sensuous, concrete and limited its first representation of these things may be, that language develops the new form and the new logical force that are continued in number.[10]

That number is the most difficult of these categories is exemplified in the dazzling variety of linguistic categories by which unity, plurality, and order in progression are expressed. Clearly, it is the latest of the logical categories to be gradually coalesced out of the heterogeneity of experience. Also, number needs the aid of a developing spatial and temporal sophistication to be freed from the qualitative. Through spatial objects, the idea of collective multiplicity — a thing and its parts — is given, and through the differentiation of temporal actions, the expression of particularity and separation — the repetition of events and actions in unbroken sequence.[11]

But even the sophistication of language expressing spatial and temporal relations cannot lead easily to the awareness that the concept of number can be used as a universal criterion of all concrete experiences. Number originates in the sense of personal uniqueness. It is fused to the elemental trinitarian relationship of I, thou, he. In addition, it must overcome the power of new qualitative experiences. Thus, it must be able to express the idea of a number system that transcends the particular world of fish, trees, turnips, and pottery. When we go from one set of concrete things to another, we need not invent a wholly new system of enumeration or classification.

Thus, in modern languages, the use of adjectives of comparison, for example, the positive, comparative, superlative, usually involves a systemic linguistic device for relating size or extent. Thus, we have great, greater, greatest, or beautiful, more beautiful, most beautiful. But others, such as good, better, best, (Latin *bonus, melior, optimus*), reflect the fact that an earlier linguistic substratum exists in which these qualitative linguistic patterns had not been supplanted by more consistently logical quantitative expressions.[12]

We can thus see space, time, and number as basic categorical constituents of natural, intuitive linguistic experience. At first indistinctly articulated and rooted in personal as well as particular sensory experiences, the actions of social life seem to release a dialectical process whereby external experience is mediated by language so as to interact with inner potentiality. Gradually, specificity and richness of relational categories are spread throughout the language and society in a widening arc of awareness. Eventually, intellectual and thus linguistic economy of expression is joined to more universal patterns of thought; and the ground is prepared for the abstract application of these constructs in socially practical areas such as architecture, land surveying, chronology, and weighing, etc.

Cassirer thus saw language assuming an evolutionary function for civilization. And while he did follow those linguistic theoreticians who saw in the various languages of man a reflection of a developmental pattern, with the modern representing a higher phase of human culture, his perspective was consistently universal. Thus, he noted the historical residues that still inhere in modern languages, such as those whose nonfunctional gender designations constitute grammatical remnants from a day when the sense of sexual distinctiveness had some mythic utility and was thus projected into language.

All peoples can travel the road to civilization, a state where they throw off the shackles of momentary feelings that enmesh the mind in the variable stream of events. The path to scientific knowledge and philosophical speculation can be carved out of the widening arc of social experiences that exposes traditional linguistic expression to the challenge of new categories of behavior and experience. The inner dialectic between thought and language will then do its work in leading a society toward conditions conducive to a broader intellectual grasp of experience.

What Cassirer argued is that an analysis of the grammatical structure of recent and historically accessible languages reveals in their formal structure a parallel evolution manifest in culture itself. Although it is certainly evident in the work of comparative linguistics that languages show evolutionary trends in phonemic structure and vocabulary, Cassirer went further; he argued that the ordinary natural language, subject as it has been to enormous accidental as well as conscious social changes, has evolved over the centuries into a more perfect instrument for logical thought.

To this end, he put forth a tentative classification of languages that reflects this universal trend toward more abstract relational categories. His argument was that the language of intuitive commonsense experience in simpler societies is limited in its range of meanings by the character of its individual words and sentences. Insofar as they denote a limited range of action and meaning, we do have a complex mesh of diverse and parallel radii of signification. Ideas are continuously conjured up and die away to be replaced by new words and images. In this earliest or mimetic stage of language formation, we can "form" collective, but not truly generic, unities. The totality of linguistic expression here attained is only an aggregate but not an articulated system; the power of articulation has exhausted itself in the individual appellation and is not adequate to the formation of comprehensive units.[13]

At this stage, one might say that sound or phonetic nuance follows meaning into an almost inexhaustible plethora of detail. Cassirer, following Otto Jespersen, noted the extraordinary range of details linguistically noted, with regard to spatial activities in American Indian languages, while at the same time the absence in these and many other cultures of generic terms for colors. But, if in this most rudimentary structural stage, perceptual experience is followed by phoneme and morpheme with discrete faithfulness, the next stage of development is hardly the logical breakthrough that might be expected.

Phase two Cassirer called the "analogical," which we find represented in a number of fairly advanced cultures. The languages of Indochina, Sudan, Ethiopia, and Finland still utilize gradations in spoken inflection to indicate alterations of meaning. True, we already have languages here incorporating more economical grammatical means. Yet a remnant of the past, the utilization of purely sensuous means — alterations of pitch and stress — are crucial for conveying the exact meaning. Yet these auditory facets of meaning are themselves conventional. Thus, a higher or lower pitch is not irrevocably fixed in any sensory signification. It does not connote height, size, or emphasis.

From the plethora of words in proto-Indo-European that means a variety of "going" comes the generic expression. From the variety of words such as "peering", "looking", "spying", "watching", eventually comes a word "seeing", that now encompasses the general case. In all languages, the vestiges point the direction toward grammars that reflect an inner tendency to classify. Whether it is the classifying suffix "ter," that joins father, mother, sister, and other family relationships into the linguistic net, or the Bantu system of "locative" prefixes, which constitutes a system of spatial relations among objects important to this culture, systemic trends in language structure force their way into all dimensions of usage.

There is here a problem in Cassirer's exposition. He noted that as far back as we go, we find elements of structural consistency in all languages. Thus, even in those languages with a multitude of particular verbs and nouns and relatively indistinct conceptions of abstract space, time, and number, there is grammatical coordination and a larger lexical and phonemic system. The particularity of linguistic experience, the transitoriness of ideas and meanings must be a surface semantic one. Deep down, a system of linguistic organization — grammar, vocabulary, phonemes — constitutes the element of permanence that holds the cultural conventions of the group together.

What makes a language rich in particulars and deprived of generic concepts is its users' sociocultural experience. The nineteenth-century linguist H. Osthoff stated it simply, "Just as man's physical eye differentiates most sharply what is closest to him in space, his spiritual eye, whose mirror is language, will most sharply differentiate and individualize those things of the perceptual world which stand closest to his feeling and thoughts, which most intensely grip his soul and excite his psychic interest, whether as an individual or a people.''[14] To the extent that the individual view of life gradually gives way to more complex social difrerentiations, to that extent the inner economy of thought is able the more easily to make its impact felt in language. This process of generic classification tends to stabilize the process of social change and could act as a dialectical pivot for the next phase of sociolinguistic advance.

III   *Language as a Symbolic Form*[15]

Neither language nor thought is reducible to the other. Language is a unique medium through which thought becomes manifest. But language, though it is the basic form of human communication, contains within itself a substantiality, whether vocal, auditory or visual (written), that determines how thought will be expressed. It is a symbolic form insofar as it carves out a unique domain in which structure and meaning are held in a dynamic, if dialectical, tension.

The form of language is given by the structure of our vocal chords and the possibilities inherent in audition (hearing). As we know, the range of phonetic expression is vast. But linguists tell us that all languages carve from this extensive range of possibilities and their consequent systems of sounds about twenty to fifty phonemes per language in which to render their meanings. Perhaps we can note the difficulty in disentangling the dynamic and sometimes confusing language systems of undeveloped societies, in terms of their transitional cultural evolution. Is a language "that" way because of lacks in sociocultural development? Can we distinguish between mimetic, analogical, and symbolic structures in language as possibly being of equal status in linguistic evolution were we to accept the principle of equality in the development of civilization — a true cultural relativism?

These are difficult issues even today. The Chomskian question as to the universality of transformational grammatical categories is now being debated with great intensity. The issue throws some light on Cassirer's view of language as a symbolic form. While he granted the structural reality of primitive languages, he did lay emphasis on the ability of language systems to purify themselves of certain patterns and gradually to attain a systematic internal form. The end of linguistic development is achieved to the extent that a grammar sheds its *ad hoc* character and expels eclecticism.

The importance to Cassirer's view of language of the systematization and morphological purification of its structure is shown by his discussion of Chinese. At first, under the prestigious influence of Wilhelm von Humboldt's view of the logical superiority of the Indo-European languages, the analysis of the so-called isolation languages, such as Chinese, where word order rather than the form of the word indicates its grammatical character, gave negative evaluations of the status of this language. Theorists in language looked upon Chinese as a formless language. And as such, it was at first seen as a representative of a supposedly early stage in man's linguistic evolution, since language was thought to evolve through a process which began with the creation of root monosyllabic words, then the parts of speech, subsequently fusing together into a sentential order. Gradually it became apparent that evidence still existed in Chinese of an earlier agglutinative stage (a one word sentence — now considered more primitive) as well as inflectional forms, of which Indo-European is a prominent example.

However, further analysis showed that in Chinese, through the logical device of word order, a highly articulated expression of grammatical relations is carried out but without the usual material grammatical means — special relational words and affixes. Even Humboldt was moved to admit this morphological integrity: the less outer grammar Chinese language seems to possess, the more inner grammar inheres in it. As Cassirer noted admiringly, "So strict indeed is this inner structure that Chinese syntax has been said to consist essentially in the logical development of a few basic laws, from which all special applications can be derived by pure logical deduction."[16]

When one examines the surface structure of such a grammar, the refinement and system implicit in it need not necessarily be found. Cassirer noted how, as with young children, word order of primitive peoples often is associated with loosely coordinated sets of ideas, clauses, and sentences.[17] One could state that in Chinese the inner grammatical form of the language has been highly refined so that thought could be freed of all material substrata and limitations. And indeed, when we realize that this trend must have been facilitated by the transition of Chinese from an exclusively spoken language to one whose written form has now long been codified and set, the advance over primitive forms can be understood. Written Chinese became primarily a vehicle for scholars. The logographs that constituted its profusion of symbols of meaning even as they increased its difficulty for the novice, did expand its range and subtlety for thought. Can one say that, in classical Chinese, thought strives to overcome the symbolic form of language by adopting a special and purified morphology in which the material appurtenances of grammar are suppressed in favor of a closely and tacitly coordinated structure of meanings?

There is evidence that Cassirer would agree that this is the case. His analysis of the polysynthetic class of languages so different from Chinese seems to reflect the view that the more compressed the meaning is in terms of linguistic simplicity the greater is its logical power for relational thought. Thus, by contrast, writes Cassirer,

In the so-called 'polysynthetic languages' the combinatory impulse seems very much predominant, expressing itself above all in the striving to represent the functional unity of linguistic meaning, materially and outwardly in a highly complex but self-contained *"phonetic configuration."* The whole of the meaning is pressed into a single word-sentence where it appears, as it were, encased in a rigid shell. But this unity of linguistic expression is not yet a true unity of thought, since it can only be achieved at the expense of the logical *"universality"* of this expression. The more modifiers the word-sentence acquires by incorporation of whole words and particles, the better it serves for the designation of a particular concrete situation, which it seeks exhaustively to detail but which it cannot connect with other similar situations to form a comprehensive general context.[18]

The advance of the symbolic form of language is thus related to its advance in providing for the expression of relational categories. And in this, the Indo-European (called Indo-Germanic) languages with inflected grammatical forms also show significant advance. But it is interesting to note the possible impact that written language had on this evolution. Language by "sight" has the capabilities of showing far more clearly the implicit structural characteristics of the language. In that sense, the written form is far more resistant to expressive or intuitive changes; it will evolve more slowly, but will do so in a far more conscious manner.

We do not know what stage of verbal expression in terms of its morphological character early Sumerian had attained before it began to be utilized in its written form. The adaptation of the cuneiform orthography by new tribes having different spoken languages has probably impeded this kind of study. However, it can be seen how Greek was gradually refined over the centuries, especially after Homer, as the written language took on a primary role as a self-conscious means of expression of the larger cultural life of the Greeks. The simplification of sentences and the elimination of modifying clauses necessitate a tighter temporal coordination of ideas. The logic becomes more explicit as the language becomes more economical.[19] Likewise, in English, as Cassirer noted, significant evolution over the past centuries has increasingly transformed the early inflected forms to a less inflected state. Words are simplified and sentences more clearly coordinated. It is difficult to know to what extent the evolution and gradual domination of writing have contributed to this trend.

With regard to language as a symbolic form, we can with Cassirer make some hypotheses and raise some questions. The advance of society and the refining of language takes place as a parallel and coordinated trend. Yet, in terms of the actual formal character of each domain, there seems to be independence of material means. No necessary relationship exists between social structure and the structure of language — phonetics, grammar, and general morphology.

Certain societies and their respective spoken language systems reach a stage where writing is attained. And, if one society seems to have first made the breakthrough, others are quick to follow. But not all are capable of doing so or will independently act to create a system of writing. Written language tends to distill the internal structure of language so that it becomes a more powerful tool of thought. The creative, expressive, metaphorical dimension that dominates the oral mode is discipliend by the written. In some cases, such as Chinese, the extreme conservatism of the written forms as well as their almost exclusively cerebral social usage causes a separation with the spoken form. Independent dialects spring up that are roughly coordinated to the written form.

At a certain point, the written form begins to generate truly conceptual forms — philosophy, religion, sciences, and mathematics. Especially in religion and philosophy, the suggestive power of the abstract concept or word tends to be extrapolated into a new reality. A tension exists between formal and substantive reality.[20] For instance, Socrates criticized the commonsense use of language as a means of rationalizing political behavior. Instead he proposed to establish a constant and logical frame of reference. As Cassirer phrased it: "And indeed, historically speaking, the problem of the concept was discovered when men learned not to accept the 'linguistic' expression of concepts as definitive, but to interpret them as 'logical questions.'"[21] Some have argued that language, especially the Indo-European languages, Greek as well as modern German, have prevented thought from freeing itself from substantive metaphysical sorts of hypostatization.

To an extent, Cassirer would agree. The purest forms of rational thought are expressed in mathematical terms. The symbolic form that is language is an imperfect means for pure thought. To the extent that thought attempts to use language, as in philosophy or theology, to go beyond the material, the sensory, or the particular, it must fail. It will entangle itself in its own antinomies. Perhaps the failure of Christian theology and Hegelian metaphysics is caused by the fact that man has here demanded too much of language for the expression of thought.

Perhaps, also, this may be the explanation why recently the Chinese have begun to abandon their traditional orthography and adopt an alphabetical structure, as is in use in the West. One wonders if in order to achieve their social and political ends, the Chinese now need a linguistic structure more easily accessible to the masses than the highly refined intellectual and aesthetic nuances of a complex logography. A simpler structure that more closely approaches the spoken language and provides easy access for all the dialects will probably be developed.

In his final comment in *The Philosophy of Symbolic Forms, I* Cassirer hinted at this interesting problem. He also gave confirmation to the proposition that language is not merely a vehicle for thought, nor is it thought itself. Rather, he declared, it is a unique human creation for the expression of symbolic meanings, having infinite possibilities for growth and change, and yet with some real limitations: "the characteristic meaning of language is not contained in the opposition between the two extremes of the sensuous and the intellectual, because in all its achievements and in every particular phase of its progress, language shows itself to be 'at once' a sensuous and an intellectual form of expression."[22]

IV   *Language and Myth*

Outside language lie forms of symbolic representation that perhaps may not even depend for the depth of their inner development on language. Certainly, the arts of painting, architecture, and other visual forms, including toolmaking, have a long evolution, perhaps independent, if parallel, to language development. One could venture the hypothesis that music and dance also are not dependent on the depth of articulation of thought in language for their possible evolution, although one could argue that the development of musical notation, impossible without the idea of written language, was a key element in the evolution of higher forms of musical expression.

At any rate, it is difficult to go beyond the above nonlinguistic forms of human expression to find linguistically independent patterns of human behavior. Language, while not all of thought, is a key human dimension for the expression and development of a wide-ranging spectrum of cognitive achievements. Thus, when we focus on the problem of myth, the point of departure must be the nature of language.

In the same year that Volume 2 of *The Philosophy of Symbolic Forms* ("Mythical Thinking") was published (1925), Cassirer's important monograph, *Language and Myth,* was issued. It argued for the inner dialectic between the two forms. It concluded with a section, "The Power of Metaphor," which hinted at the evolution from language to poetry and thus art. It is the close inner relationship between language and myth that Cassirer was concerned to underline. And yet, in *Language and Myth,* this relationship is not fully comprehended — and this is also true for the first two volumes of *The Philosophy of Symbolic Forms.*

At this stage, Cassirer was clearly articulating the differences in logic and structure that separate language, seen as discursive or logical thought, from the complex, immediate interstices of mythic image. He was concerned with establishing the special and particulate character of the mythological mode of thinking and the special logic that inheres in its original inception and its subsequent evolution. It is bound to language and perception as its material substratum. But the two forms do go their own ways, expressing unique intellectual valences.

In the case of myth, Cassirer broke away from the typical rationalistic biases of the European philosophical tradition. He did not view myth as an aberrant form of philosophical thought or as a primordial phase out of which logical canons will one day evolve and, in the meantime, efface all earlier signs of the mythic experience. The existence of mythical thinking and its subsequent evolution into more recent religious modalities is due, so Cassirer argued, to an independent pattern of symbolic functioning that is inherent in thought. As such, it cannot be excepted from intellectual consideration or evaluation by pejorative comparisons.

It is in the third volume of *The Philosophy of Symbolic Forms* ("Phenomenology of Knowledge") that a broadening in the perspective on language and myth is seen. Following a sensitive discussion and critique of the phenomenologically oriented neo-Kantianism of friend and fellow Marburger Paul Natorp, *(Allgemeine Psychologie nach kritischer Methode [General Psychology in Accordance with the Critical Method], 1912),* Cassirer tried to establish the integrating principle of the various forms of cultural expression.[23] Whether one views these expressions from a subjective or an objective standpoint, what brings them into systematic relationship is not their adherence to a principle of law whereby each is similarly constructed. By turning to language and myth, one does not perceive the building up of lawlike regularities equal to the scientific structures of knowledge. Rather, the principle of unity is one of form, within which independent principles of objectivization are to be noted.

In going beyond the Kantian methodology upon which Natorp attempted to build, Cassirer argued the necessity to expand "the three dimensions of the logical, ethical, and aesthetic: it must, in particular, draw the forms of language and myth into its sphere, if it aspires to find its way back to the primary subjective sources, the original attitudes and formative modes of consciousness."[24]

The question raised by Cassirer in the third volume of *The Philosophy of Symbolic Forms* is not merely with the inner structure of language and myth, but with the relationship of the structures of perceptive, intuitive, and cognitive consciousness.[25] Now, we have not only the independence of the substantive modes of consciousness, but these particular developmental as well as relational issues.

The key distinction to be made here is between perceptive and intuitive experience. It is already understood that cognitive experience begins at that point in intellectual growth when ordinary "linguistic expressions" are not accepted as definitive, when they are interpreted as "logical questions."[26] In short, philosophy and the sciences grow out of language when the intuitive level of experiencing language is brought into wider intellectual and relational focus.

The intuitive level can be thought of as being the "logical" or "secular" domain of ordinary linguistic expression. It is itself subject to those inner structural trends that create language systems of consistent grammatical organization. Where language is able to develop class and relational concepts on an intuitive level so that a fairly high level of civilizing activities can so proceed, we have the fullest potentiality of linguistic symbolic form. Language is capable of dealing with people, things, and events in terms of causal relationships, substance, and attributes, etc.; it is in the fullest meaning of the term, commonsense discourse.

But this is an advanced state of symbolic development for language. Before this, it has had to surpass the mimetic and analogical phases. The primary mimetic stage, in which language seeks to follow perceptual experience in its immediate profusion of particularity, in its momentary emotional as well as functional needs, stands as an abstract beginning. It is difficult to conceive of language ever following a theoretically simple perceptual set of experiences. Perceptual experience already reflects, as the Gestaltists have noted, structures, faces, smiles, objects, voices.[27]

Then how do we explain the very gradual development of language at its mimetic, perceptual level, when, through its own inner logic, it should rapidly attain to a purely symbolic, if intuitive, inner as well as outward structure and mode of experiencing? The answer is that at the perceptual level of experience, these admittedly holistic and organized symbols are immersed by a more dynamic element than would be implied by the purely descriptive and formal concept "mimetic"; in other words, the mimetic stage of language is also the mythic level of expression. Thus, what we can see as a primary stage of the organization of perceptual experience for mankind, to a certain extent paralleled in the ontogenetic development of the child, Cassirer calls, more generally, the expressive level.

This expressive level is not merely a beginning for man; it shows itself in the animal world, too. The animal instinctually seizes a perceptual experience; every sound, movement, nuance, becomes to an animal a sign triggering involuntary responses. The creature does not live in a world of objective evaluation of things and events, but in a world in which each reception of a percept becomes an occasion for an expressive response.[28]

With man, the expressive moment is both voluntary and involuntary. It is the former because no strict instinctual specificities call up man's responses. On the other hand, the logic of man's response on the mythical expressive level is never clearly in view, nor is it consistent even when the same external sign or occasion seems to be repeated. According to Cassirer:

> The primary mythical fact is a man divided and torn to and fro by manifold outward impressions, each bearing a definite magical-mythical character, each laying claim to the whole of human consciousness and drawing it into its sphere, each imprinting its own color and mood. At first the ego had nothing to oppose to this impression and is unable to change it but can only accept it and in the act of acceptance become its prisoner. It is tossed this way and that by the expressive factors of the various phenomena, which assault it suddenly and irresistibly. These factors follow one another without fixed order and without transition; unpredictably, the various formations change their mythical "face." Without transition, an impression of the homelike, familiar, sheltering, and protective can shift into its opposite, the inaccessible, terrifying, monstrous, and gruesome.[29]

To understand the power of myth to define this primary expressive state in man's cognitive development, one must consider that we are here dealing with a primary psychological state, a valence of mind, an intentionality that impresses itself with irrefutable power on all the other intellectual and aesthetic potentialities of man. Language, which derives from other cognitive structural capacities in man, articulates itself in the word, the name, and thus can reflect its own intellectual need to stabilize experience. But this unique linguistic structural capability is immediately inundated by the overwhelming psychic force of the mythic or expressive attitude. And it is at first prevented from articulating its own inner phylogeny leading toward the culminating intuitive form of symbolic expression.

When we think of myth, we think of distinctions such as between man and God. But such distinctions are the product of a long intellectual struggle to bring order into perceptual experience. For, even within the expressive, there is a long road from confusion to structure. And thus, within myth, an inner dialectic eventually leads to the higher religions, declares Cassirer:

And what myth begins in this direction is completed by language and art: the god acquires full individuality only through his name [language] and image [art]. Thus the intuition of himself as a determinate, clearly delimited individual is not the starting point from which man progressively builds his general view of reality: rather, this intuition is only the end, it is only the mature fruit of a creative process in which all the diverse energies of the spirit are at work and acting reciprocally on one another.[30]

V   The Structure of Mythical Symbolism

In the concept of myth as a symbolic form, we find Cassirer's greatest move away from the orthodox neo-Kantianism of his predecessors. Because he seeks the forms of symbolic envisagement in all of human culture he breaks, for example, with Natorp's classical attempt to find a principle of law that can subsume all of logic, aesthetics, and ethics into a Kantian synthesis. Rather, the concept of form helps Cassirer bring within his systematic investigations the phenomenon of myth. Here, in this totally different realm, he sought for a structure of ideas that would more accurately reflect the realities of cultural experience. He sought to strengthen our understanding of that long historic preparation for the modern systems of intellectual creativity.

In myth, we are forced to reconsider our analysis of this evolution. The process whereby we articulate in terms of scientific accuracy such entities as substance-attribute; space, time, and number; I-thou-it; cause and consequence; is not a smooth progression. It does not move along with social development as a consequence of environmental competence. Rather, it is at all times interdicted by a terrible and powerful force of emotion and feeling. The primordial experiences of man are therefore not practical, secular, or prosaically adaptive. They are, in contrast, suffused with creative, internally motivated, qualitative factors.

And yet, as Cassirer is at great pains to develop in the second volume of *The Philosophy of Symbolic Forms,* this qualitative dimension that creates mythic symbolism has its own inner logic, which even in its primary, seemingly chaotic expressions, eventually proceeds to effect a revolution in the interaction of feeling and thought. The way upward from the realm of perceptual immediacy, pure feelings of the sensory, toward the great religious and ethical constructs of historic times is mediated by turmoil and time. Yet the dialectical process is not necessarily a retelling of a fixed cycle of beginnings and endings in human culture. The more significant meaning in Cassirer's analysis, especially as his writings conclude on the motifs of myth and culture in *The Myth of the State* (1945), is that we have a never-ending cycle of relationships in which the creative mind will always have a significant role.

If experience on the expressive level is never mundane, then the archetypal division that feeling must create for itself is the distinction between that which must be disregarded — the ordinary, the profane — and that which must be marked with emotional or mythic significance — the sacred. Along with this concept is the most universally expressed "mana" concept, that which is holy, as well as its converse, the taboo, that which is to be avoided. These divisions in expressive feeling are not imposed upon man by any principle of sensory or perceptual primacy. One cannot predict what will provide grist for the structural character of mythic experience. A whole range of objects, events, experiences, and subjective emotions can turn the world into a glistening profusion of often contradictory attitudes. Hates, fears, humility, aggression, submission all lead toward a pantheon of holy objects, often coming into being and fading out as rapidly as the wind changes its direction.

Demons, magical rites, gods, sacrifices, totems, miracles, empathic intuitions all add up to a world of qualitative richness; but in terms of the logical or even the commonsense intuitive world view, it is chaotic and without lawful regularity. And yet, Cassirer argues, it *is* a world of regularity, but ordered on different symbolic principles. Certainly, as anthropologists have richly documented, this is a world of meaning. All peoples living under the spell of mythic attitudes find it possible to order experience. Only it is not ordered according to what we understand to be socially efficacious for ourselves.

Logical distinctions between the animate and the inanimate, between natural causes and consequences are not important yet. It is possible that the mythic mind has not yet been able to attach that universal search for meaning in general to a structure of natural causal relations. Thus, Cassirer declares, the search for meaning which is characteristic of all phases of intellectual development flows out widely and inchoately:

...before the world as a whole has split into determinate, enduring, and unitary forms, there is a phase during which it exists for man only in unformed feeling. In this indeterminacy of feeling certain impressions are set off from the common background by their special intensity and force. To them correspond the first mythological images. They are not products of reflection which dwells on certain objects in order to ascertain their enduring characteristics, their constant traits, but are the expressions of a unique stirring, a momentary tension and release, of the consciousness, which will perhaps never be repeated in similar form.[31]

The state of affairs here described with typical poetic aptness by Cassirer is a limiting one. It will gradually take on more permanent form, but one that is still by and large ordered by the powerful feelingness of the expressive stage. Perceptual experience itself will provide those conditions, pivoting points around which the mythic mind will evolve. The nestling immanence of the multitude of nature demons and place gods will gradually coalesce into a more simplified if permanent and ordered pantheon of higher powers and principles. The empathic and universal life feeling, that fear of death and reverence for dynamic existence, out of which totemism is created, will gradually ritualize the kinship of man, nature, animal and society. Space, time, and number will act as pivots around which more permanent foci of social existence can be built.

Communities will have their plan of dwellings, their holy buildings and places, their burial grounds and trysting areas. Festivals with games, ritual, and magic will mark the passage of seasons, says Cassirer: "The primary mythical 'sense of phases' can apprehend time only in the image of life, and consequently it must transpose and dissolve everything which moves in time, everything which comes and goes in set rhythm, into the form of life."[32]

And finally, in the sense of the singular and the plural, the dawning awakening to the fact that objects can be classified in terms of a systemic diversity in unity is drawn at first into the sacred circle of mythic life. Because of its immanent intellectual power, number stands out as an important way station on the road to civilization. Yet, because of its mysterious significance for man, it has remained permeated with mythical qualities. Number, writes Cassirer, "...proves itself to be the bond which joins the diverse powers of consciousness into a mesh, which gathers the spheres of sensation, intuition, and feeling into a unity. Number thus fulfills the function which the Pythagoreans impute to harmony. It is 'a unity of many

mixed elements and an agreement between disagreeing elements'. . . . it acts as the magic tie which not so much links things together as brings them into harmony within the soul.''[33] Experience
centering around the individual, his awareness of others, the
various natural foci for actions, the inherent relationships which
activity calls to attention results in their acting as efficient causes in
propelling forward that fundamental dialectic in the progress of
civilization. The dual elements that are intertwined in the evolution
of the expressive stage, from the standpoint of the mythic attitude
are: (1) the search for signification and meaning that erupts out of
man's expressive demands like a torrent of water tearing the earth
as it makes its channel, and (2) the fact that man, without in-
stinctive specificity, must find this meaning in an as yet incipient or
implicit structure of thought. This form and content we can only
know in terms of their immanent character, that is, they are always
''becoming.'' Thus, while the mythic dimension of the expressive
stage may evolve into higher cognitive forms of thought, the very
fact of man's noninstinctually directed effusion of energies,
coupled with an inchoate awareness of these forces, renders him
perennially subject to the mythic mode of expression.

Cassirer emphasized that the search for a principle of divinity, a
logical source of the creative unity of the social world, is subject to
this inner logical demand of mind. Man's search to understand
both himself and nature is reflected by the gradual domination of
the principle of the godhead. The Egyptian religion is illustrative.
King Amenophis IV, about 1500 B.C., attempted to suppress the
earlier polytheistic religions by establishing the one sun god, Aton.
This god was symbolized as a disk sending out rays from all sides,
each ray ending in a hand that holds out the symbol of life. Here is
an expression of a new principle of diversity in which all humanity
can participate. The new hymns, which speak of ethical and metaphysical ideals, surpass the old magical cults, rituals, myths, and
talismans. Now, all the peoples of the empire can join in to praise
the ultimate source of reality and power. The human mind, coming
to terms with its own capacity to integrate experience, has cast out
an older, rich, but formless religious domain and has attempted to
enter a new phase of the symbolic form of feeling.[34]

One can attempt to draw this dividing line between the world of
myth and the development of religion by focusing on the strictly
logical difference between the two. The experiences, the constants

of life and the environment remain the same. Man's instinctual deprivation, his aloneness in the world, the powerful emotions that wash over him and often efface his logical potentialities also remain the same. What is different is man's capacity, through the development of his logical awareness, to confront these emotions and for the first time attempt to direct them into psychologically and socially useful condensations of symbolic meaning. Man need not become an animal to empathize with nature. The tree hit by lightning need not be a god, nor the spot where a loved one died become forever defiled and taboo.

Man is now able to make the distinction between the symbol of his concern and the meaning that he attaches to that symbol. The two logical states are not merged into each other, Cassirer argues: "Religion takes the decisive step that is essentially alien to myth: in its use of sensuous images and signs it recognizes them as such — a means of expression which, though they reveal a determinate meaning, must necessarily remain inadequate to it, which 'point' to this meaning but never wholly exhaust it."[35]

Cassirer spoke of an inner dialectic of the mythical consciousness: "... it reaches a turning point at which the law that governs it becomes a problem...";[36] and "... in completing its own cycle it ends by breaking through it."[37] What is it that causes this dialectical process that lifts thought onto a new plane of apprehension, whereby myth is transformed into religion? The image, the perception of that expressive moment, the material of awareness that was first joined with its meaning is now of a sudden separated into a conventional symbolic relationship.

Cassirer did not say explicitly how this separation is achieved. The suggestions are widely enough distributed in his various writings such that a brief reconstruction of the meaning and substance of this most epochal moment in mythic form is possible. "This fulfillment which is at the same time a transcendence..."[38] must result from a dialectical process that is broader and more far reaching for man than myth or religion itself. It is of the same sort of evolution as occurs in language, and Cassirer recognizes it as such.[39]

The question then arises over the dialectic that carries both language and myth beyond the expressive level to the intuitive or representative levels and ultimately to truly conceptual thinking, a purely inner-directed process. Are the laws and trends automatically given to man? If so, how can we account for the diversity of levels in human culture and therefore the diversity of time tables for this historic process?

There can be no doubt that the specifically logical character of this process is seen as being an internal one, in the manner of the process of intellectual growth, as proferred by the Piagetian school of "developmental epistemology." But, on the other hand, the conditions of social use for myth or language are important factors in understanding the material conditions that release or inhibit the inner dialectic of reason.

Language transcends the mimetic and analogical stages of the sensuous union of sound and meaning to reach a conventional level where the relationship of sound and symbol is increasingly determined by the inner grammatical structure and the harmonious interaction of the parts to the whole. Here, we see the evolution of language on an intuitive level of representation, conditioned as it is by almost unconscious formal relationships. The final step to be taken by language is, as we have noted before, to have this intuitive structure of meaning, or of common sense, itself questioned. Here, we see the relative secularity of intuitive representations put to a higher and more inclusive universality of philosophical and scientific inquiry — cognition.

The transition from myth to religion takes place somewhat differently. For, while the "transcendence" toward religion constitutes a great logical leap of mind, religion *qua* religion remains joined to mythic form by its inability to break from its expressive emotional sources. Language may be the root form of philosophy and science, which can and does create new materials of intellectual discourse, metaphysics, chemistry, and mathematics. But religion can never fully separate itself from its basic material categories — the holy objects, the mystical unifications, the tabooed objects and behaviors, the festivals, shrines, rituals of the mythic world. For to separate itself thus would be for it to abandon its own inner nature and become, as some religions did in the eighteenth-century Enlightenment, a religion of reason (unitarianism), which was more a philosophy than a religion.

The switch from the purely mythical point of view to the religious attitude is not a neat and unequivocal event. The evolution of Greek and Roman mythology is an example. In the most ancient stratum of Roman "religion," we can still see the remnants of those impersonal gods of the moment, gods of place and function. More advanced are "the gods of the flame on the hearth," the sacred centers of family and home life. In the Greek "religion," this relatively impersonal level of family and ancestor worship can barely be discerned.

The gods of historic time are personal gods, having human attributes. They are not gods of morality; rather, they represent, as Cassirer put it, "mental ideals."[40] In their humanness, they became centers of various personal allegiances and affections. The philosophers may have decried their deeds and general deportment; yet they were a developed pantheon of mythological attributes, without ever having risen to the prophetic moral vision of the monotheistic, pantheistic, and ethical religions of the East. Could it be that in this last hesitation to make a transcendent leap from the "mythological" to the religious, the Greek culture was able to carve out a place in its linguistic view of experience for science and philosophy? Can we hypothesize that the emancipation of the aesthetic dimension in Greek culture — in architecture, painting, music, and poetry — was made possible by the flexibility of the mythic domain?

We cannot know for sure. But certainly, the reality of the interaction of symbolic forms with each other is given a certain amount of force in the fact that Greek religious and philosophical motifs both infiltrated Roman cultural life. And parallel with the decline of the pagan religious tradition and the dominance of the Christians, the Eastern schismatics from Judaism, there also occurred the decline and absorption into Christianity of what remained of the Greek philosophical tradition.

The permeability of the logical membrane that separates each of the forms, the religious and the philosophical, reflects the fact that in the higher religions, we have exemplified a more significant developmental difference between myth and religion than exists in language, where Cassirer postulated three stages — mimetic (expressive), intuitive (ordinary language), and cognitive (philosophy or science). The examples that Cassirer gave in the second volume of *The Philosophy of Symbolic Forms* are Buddhism, Judaism, and Zoroastrianism, all of which have significant ethical elements.

Whereas the simpler mythological forms have gods and rituals that are impersonal and in flux, the Greeks created a pantheon of gods that are human and reflect the perennial qualities and characteristics of man. The eastern religious traditions go beyond what is, to what should be. They demand that man look upon the highest principle as an abstract set of values not reflective of material or sensible things. Thus, we have, according to Cassirer, the great Judaic aversion to graven images, the war against the more primitive human motive:

> In the prophetic books of the Old Testament we find an entirely new direction of thought and feeling. The ideal of purity means something quite different from all the former mythical conceptions. To seek for purity or impurity in an object, in a material thing, has become impossible. Even human actions, as such, are no longer regarded as pure or impure. The only purity that has religious significance and dignity is purity of the heart.[41]

Although as Cassirer noted repeatedly, there can never be a complete break between myth and religion, there is a shift in vision in the motives or intentions that direct the individual to new concerns: for example, a more abstract awareness of principles and essences. These engage the mind along with the empathic or expressive elements. The sense of the holy or of a higher principle of reality that is god constitutes a basic awareness of the dependency of man on these higher forces, forces that Friedrich Schleiermacher took to be the universal cause of religion. All of these are transmuted from the concrete immediacy of the mythic to principles that engage either ethical, metaphysical, or sociohistorical constructs. To the extent that religions attempt to pass through their essential character into these realms, they lay themselves open to being supplanted by new and more vigorous, even if more primitive, mythicoreligious evocations.

One can understand the power of Christianity over the centuries. This religion has striven to incorporate into its structure a complex blend of elements of the magical, ritualistic, and cultish alongside supremely refined ethical, metaphysical, and sometimes mystical elements. Its power to adapt to the new resides in the fact that it has never lost its contact with those mysterious expressive dimensions of the human condition. Yet, at the same time, at its upper reaches of symbolic meaning, it has opened itself up to new philosophical, social, and political movements. By keeping the mysteries of the faith close to the mythic needs of the ordinary individual, it has maintained its contact with the primeval energies of human existence. Yet, as in Thomism, it is able to transmit a metaphysical and ethical message that challenges the most refined secular philosophical doctrines.

Thus through the refining of the special refractory lens that shapes the human heart and mind to the mythico-religious mode, the long-term force of this symbolic form is revealed. Cassirer argued that the import of a symbolic form can only be fully disclosed when what might be called the psychological intentions of the form, in this case feeling or expressivity, or even an instinctless sense of dependency in man, can be logically distanced from the object of symbolization, whether they be material or ideational.

The capacity to reflect equally on a word in its objective, religious, or aesthetic import is given to man only gradually. He must distill each of these valences of mind into its proper channel. And this capacity of man to rise to the truly representational level of mind, to consider and evaluate meanings in spite of the power of emotional forces that would act to join meaning and object in momentary expressive spontaneity, characterizes the uniqueness of the symbolics of culture. Only when we perceive the distance that each of the forms, especially myth and religion, has gone to attain its refined cultural power can we perceive and understand the treasure that is high culture and thus the continuing mystery that inheres in man's basic spiritual nature.

The question still remains: once attained, how far can man regress? And, of course, we know of the struggle in which religious leaders, from the Jewish prophets to the various saints, have had to engage to prevent their people from slipping back to the primitive modalities from which they have often been unwillingly dragged. To this issue Cassirer returned after many years of intense work in the outer reaches of the epistemologies of the physical sciences and the history of modern philosophy.[42]

VI   Myth in Modern Society

Shortly after Cassirer arrived in the United States in 1941, he was bombarded with questions concerning the meaning of what was happening in a world that literally was being torn to bits. He had had to leave Germany in 1933, had lived in England, then in Sweden before coming to teach at Yale University in 1941. He had been a victim of fascism. Before his eyes, the Nazis had conjured up a whole series of images, rituals, and slogans, which must have reminded him of what he had written about with regard to myth in the 1920s.

He was deeply concerned with what had happened to that deeply rooted and soaringly intellectual culture of Germany in which he had been nurtured. How could it have collapsed into the intellectual mire that was Nazi Germany? How could such a society, with educational, cultural, and scientific institutions second to none, so quickly be transformed into a nation whose citizens tolerated a level of officially sponsored bestiality that had no precedent in history?

As he considered these issues, especially since he had lived through the social turmoil of the twenties, which anticipated the crisis of Weimar Germany in the early 1930s, he began to plan an essay that would deal with these difficult questions. But first, there was the necessity of preparing a statement for the English-speaking world on his basic philosophical position as given in *The Philosophy of Symbolic Forms*. These volumes, then still untranslated from the German, were probably too abstract for the average American student of philosophy. Thus *An Essay on Man* (1944) was written in English by Cassirer to serve not only as a summary of *The Philosophy of Symbolic Forms* but as an advanced, if brief, rendering on his outlook as it had evolved over the years.

The next task, on which he started immediately after completing *An Essay on Man,* progressed to the point of being printed in abbreviated from in *Fortune Magazine* in June, 1944. The *Myth of the State,* as it was then and in book form entitled, was completed in manuscript shortly before Cassirer's sudden death in April, 1945, and published under the editorship of Yale colleague, Charles Hendel, in 1946.

The book presented a special challenge for Cassirer, for he here had to leave the abstract realms of history and theory to inquire in concrete detail into the living dynamics of the problem of symbolic form. His usual approach had been to draw from the details of the historical, ethnological, and empirical the materials that could be woven into his fabric of theory. Now he had to examine a disquieting rupture in Western culture, to place those elements that had boiled up from below, and hold both the ideal and the real together in a context of dynamic tensions.

Cassirer's approach was to examine the issue of myth from the standpoint of its ethnological as well as psychological origin and ramifications, including an interesting discussion of Freudianism, and then develop the theory of the state, in its historical evolution. He attempted to show how the mythic and the rational in a sense were competing elements in the evolution of the philosophy of society. He was clear on the desire to liberate human society from mythical elements, to live according to law. He also showed how at many points political leaders, even theoreticians, were wont to inject mythical elements into the state. One might say that the subversion of reason inhered in the failure of reason to be able properly to distinguish those elements of social life that could be subsumed in justice and law and those that ought to be subject to more personal and emotional influences. The modern political myths, Cassirer argued, were created in times of great emotional stress, and their capacity to break through the structure of civilized life was prepared for in the heretofore incomplete victory of the rational principle. Because of the existence of intellectuals who intervened in favor of ideals that could be perverted by the likes of fascism, the weakness of the modern democratic state would remain apparent.

But the actual methodologies of the Nazi state do reveal in the concrete what can be understood to be a paradigmatic set of actions that undermined the concrete structure of democratic life. It is not enough to utilize the ideas of a Machiavelli, Carlyle, Hegel, and Gobineau as an intellectual smoke screen to subvert the fragile structure of parliamentary democracy. As Aristotle once pointed out, a political system must be lived before it can be written up and enacted. So, too, to create a new political order, national socialism first would have to throw down the very fabric of republican life.

The use of mythic techniques to obtain their ends was an intuitively successful stroke on the part of Hitler and his cohorts. It clearly reflects the vulnerability of civilizations, and it lends a chastening note to the optimism that is at the core of Cassirer's philosophy and that in part detracts from its impact in our own tenuous era. Nevertheless, *The Myth of the State* both explicitly and implicitly demonstrates the tangible truth of Cassirer's *The Philosophy of Symbolic Forms*.

Language and myth constitute the mammoth trunk of cultural symbolism. Everywhere in every society the evidence is deep, rich, and pervasive. This is our cultural heritage. In these phenomena, language and myth, our human search for meaning, expressivity, and release were shaped in far-reaching diversity as well as held together in this universal form. Only through a great deliberative distillation of experience were the logical threads of language and myth disentangled and the inner formal nature of each enabled to develop in terms of its own particular inner logic. To do this, there had to be a reciprocal development in the social and technological side of experience. Even tools, as Cassirer noted, on the primitive and mythological level first seen as organic projections of man's body, later had to be conceived as prosaically functional things and allowed to evolve in terms of these functional needs.

Certainly freeing language from the constraints of mythic attitudes allowed it to be shaped to its representative function. The grammatical and syntactical ordering of relationships is no doubt reflected in social developments and these were ultimately preparatory to the creation of written languages. The interaction of language with myth can be seen in the gradual refinement of mythic structures both in Egypt and in Greece. These early religions laid the groundwork for the quasi-philosophical perspectives contained in the monotheistic religions of the first millenium B.C.

From this stem grows art, seen as a form in itself, and then philosophy, science, and history. The symbolic capacity of man to create relational forms stretching over the breadth of culture, yet building in the direction of cognition, ideality, discipline, and logical purity are motifs of a struggle of the human mind to actualize itself. The significant psychological motivations that fuel the refinement and growth of culture still exist, as in myth and art. But they are carefully tuned to the variegated experiences of man as he attempts vigorously to introduce "sense into his sensations."

Political forms of social life are themselves created both from the theoretical and ideological environment of possibilities and from the contemporary fabric of symbolic experience. Periclean Athens is an example. Here, the aesthetic, ethical, religious, and technological envisionment of life all contributed to that momentary flourishing of democracy. The basic shape of mythic fears and dependencies remains with the human condition. But the firm web of cultural institutions and intellectual achievements weaken the danger of the nihilistic abandonment of civilization for any momentary union with the symbols of life and death. It is almost as if the creative symbolic thrust in culture acts to combat the dissolutions of regressive infantile dependency.

The tenuous social and political conditions of Germany, the incipient fears of the masses, socially separated as they were from the intellectuals, made the masses easy prey to the techniques of mythic manipulation.[43] The great defect of this democratic government was that it had not dug its roots — intellectual, cultural, as well as political — deeply into the lives of the people. This situation allowed the Nazis to rally the masses around those more tangible and expressive symbols of meaning — the swastika, the goosestep, the brown shirt. But these were merely the accoutrements to a more basic negative theme — fear and hate. Here was the myth of racial superiority and inferiority, the sense of alienation of a people from the rest of humanity and the stigmatization of defilement toward the Jews. Add to this the sense of historic abuse felt by the German people, the shame of defeat in earlier wars, the unjust advantage their neighbors had taken of them, the dismemberment of the "fatherland," and we have a demonology of powerful, mythical efficacy.

Cassirer spoke about the use of language that is torn from its neutral secular function (intuitive language) and degraded to a new mythic level:

...I find to my amazement that I no longer understand the German language. New words have been coined; and even the old ones are used in a new sense; they have undergone a deep change of meaning. This change of meaning depends upon the fact that those words which formerly were used in a descriptive, logical, or semantic sense are now used as magic words that are destined to produce certain effects and to stir up certain emotions. Our ordinary words are charged with meanings; but these new-fangled words are charged with feelings and violent passions.[44]

The two major forms of cultural ascent, language and myth, are irrevocably linked. The mythmakers of our era know that they cannot destroy secular reason through the visual symbols of hatred and fear. Their rhetoric is also laughable unless they can degrade the common coinage of ordinary linguistic discourse. And thus the introduction of magic words, states Cassirer:

But the skillful introduction of the magic word is not all. If the word is to have its full effect it has to be supplemented by the introduction of new rites. In this respect, too, the political leaders proceeded very thoroughly, methodically, and successfully. Every political action has its special ritual. And since, in the totalitarian state, there is no private sphere, independent of political life, the whole life of man is suddenly inundated by a high tide of new rituals. They are as regular, as rigorous and inexorable as those rituals that we find in primitive societies.[45]

Cassirer noted the implacable fear that those who attempt to manipulate the totalitarian state have of the free exercise of reason or creativity in any cultural area. Just as writing was a critical step in the broadening of the human consciousness in religion, the arts, philosophy, and science, so great intellectual achievement in any one particular symbolic form inevitably radiates laterally to stimulate other modalities of creative enterprise. Thus, great social eras have been great creative eras, and we note this in the history of culture when we look at the Greek Golden Age, the Augustan Age in Rome, the Renaissance, or the baroque and romantic periods of Europe, and their equivalents in the Eastern civilizations, whether Muslim, Hindu, or Chinese. The totalitarian state, whether run by the Hitlerites or Stalinists, invariably acts to destroy the independence and creative work of all cultural endeavors. But in doing so, they of course signal and precipitate a process of atrophy that must eventually destroy them also.

In Cassirer's analysis of the work of myth in destroying the social structure of a civilized people, there is a critical question: in what way is the modern political myth unique in the history of civilization? What does its peculiarly violent character signify? In returning to such primordial human emotional concerns, linked as myth is with a technological capacity of unprecedented power, does it now represent a special turn in the development of civilized life? A pregnant insight is apparent in his analysis, one which is left undeveloped but is still of special significance in that Cassirer saw the modern totalitarian society as constituting a sharp break with the past:

Methods of compulsion and supression have ever been used in political life. But in most cases these methods aimed at material results. Even the most fearful systems of despotism contented themselves with forcing upon men certain laws of action. They were not concerned with the feelings, judgments, and thoughts of men. It is true that in the great religious struggles the most violent efforts were made not only to rule the actions of men but also their consciousness. But these attempts were bound to fail, they only strengthened the feeling for religious liberty. Now the modern political myths proceeded in quite a different manner. They did not begin with demanding or prohibiting certain actions. They undertook to change the men, in order to be able to regulate and control their deeds. The political myths acted in the same way as a serpent that tries to paralyze its victims before attacking them. Men fell victims to them without any serious resistance. They were vanquished and subdued before they had realized what actually happened.[46]

Cassirer was himself not insensitive to the fact that the mythic element lives on in culture—in religion, art, and language. In his analysis in *The Myth of the State* he recognized in the psychoanalytic work of Sigmund Freud the contemporary over-tones of the "expressive" dimension. It here persisted in the psychodynamics of our own inner personal lives. And while he praised Freud for recognizing the depths of the problem of culture as well as individuality—the source from which these tumultuous human "lustrative" forces ascend—yet he still saw only the earlier Freud, the architect of the libido theory and the reductive per-spectives on   sexuality.[47]

But, as Susanne Langer has pointed out, there is much on which Cassirer and Freud would agree had their intellectual paths crossed earlier.[48] The vast realm that Freud lays out in his morphology of the unconscious, of dream and phantasy, of regression and in-fantile thinking, all approach the position that Cassirer developed in his various writings on myth.[49] This awareness that Freud gave us, enabling us to obtain access to the unconscious, showing us that this vast domain that had been thought to have been paved over by a veneer of culture and rationalism could still be released from its entombment, was a powerfully suggestive social cue.

In earlier periods of history, cultures warred against each other as equals, as challengers for the leadership of civilization. It did not occur to one religious or philosophical persuasion to dissolve opposition by the use of techniques of brainwashing, propaganda, and bizarre mythologies. Perhaps it was a tacit recognition by all contending ideologies that the mask of civilization was hard won. Woe to those who tampered with it, as with Pandora's box. It could consume them as well.

But in our modern world, with a dominant sociotechnological structure that has swept away all previous contenders, a smugness about the security of civilization has set in. Added to this are the vast masses of people who have left the cultural security of rural and small-town life for the dynamic adventure of modernity. Anxiety and fear now open them up to new and ultimate exploitations. The new totalitarians, themselves uprooted from traditional religious, cultural, and ethical restraints, dazzled by the enormous power at their fingertips, have nothing to fear from the contamination of myth. They themselves do not represent a culture, an ethical tradition, or religion. They are functionaries, in whom the banality of power is frighteningly exemplified.

In language and myth, Cassirer saw the beginnings of a great symbolic edifice of culture. In our own twentieth century it constituted an open-ended creative endeavor, a living and exhilarating monument to the mystery of human thought. In logic, mathematics, philosophy, and the arts, the quest for significant meaning reflected the rich essence of the possibilities of the human spirit. Yet now, in his last years, Cassirer encountered a new theme which seemed to announce a new dialectical antithesis, a return of culture to its primeval origins. At the very end of *The Myth of the State*, he recognized the paradox, but could not answer for it:

> The world of human culture...could not arise until the darkness of myth was fought and overcome. But the mythical monsters were not entirely destroyed. They were used for the creation of a new universe, and they still survive in this universe. The powers of myth were checked and subdued by superior forces. As long as these forces, intellectual, ethical, and artistic, are in full strength, myth is tamed and subdued. But once they begin to lose their strength chaos is come again. Mythical thought then starts to rise anew and to pervade the whole of man's cultural and social life.[50]

VII Art

Language and myth remain as the root symbolic forms. Out of their unity of feeling and expression are gradually extruded the higher and more independent modalities, of which art is one of the first to announce itself to the human consciousness. It is not true to say that art does not exist at the earliest historic moments or on the simplest cultural levels. Cassirer pointed out that in all magical ceremonialism and ritual, there is also picture magic.[51] And, of course, decoration, dancing, music, chant, and rhythms are indissolubly joined to language and myth.

But, as in early language usage and mythic symbols, a self-conscious awareness of the aesthetic attitude and of art as a unique approach to experience is lacking. This unity of cultural attitudes inundates and obliterates what we are later able to uncover as independent creative possibilities in experience. What Cassirer called the "expressive" level of consciousness is a rich amalgam of emotional and experiential factors. But it is a period in cultural history in which this richness is subject to the shifting fits and starts of the moment, the sense of the social norm, the taboo, the fears, and last, the rigidities that eventually paralyze the primitive expressive consciousness and inhibit its evolution toward self-conscious independence.

But this view already raises some serious questions. For art is radically unlike the other symbolic forms. It is, for example, more different from the logical or discursive intellectual forms than is myth or religion. Eventually, mythic patterns, despite their perennial involvement in that emotional sense of human weakness and limits, are infused with higher order transmutations of these themes in ethical or metaphysical expression. But art stays with the particular or concrete, with the sensuous and the material. It does not necessitate higher levels of science or philosophy or even great technological or cultural work to bring forth its unique modal vision of experience.

The cave art of Altamira and Lescaux is an interesting challenge to the implicit developmental view of Cassirer. Here, twenty to twenty-five thousand years ago, early men painted subtle recreations of experience. The dynamic of these living forms is expressed in a way that contemporary artists respect as a true aesthetic creation of reality. Now, it may be that the intent of these artists was secular, to imitate or copy nature, their memorized impressions of the outer world transferred to the dark, interior walls. It could be that the overt intentions were religious or ritualistic; they could have been created to celebrate in visual form certain sacred meanings or moments during the year. Whatever the purported rationale for these wall paintings, what did come forth was a manifestation of a unique artistic sense. Can one then argue that the emancipation of art from the grasp of myth has actually taken place in a strict chronological progression?

The freedom that Katharine Gilbert would like to see for art must be carefully analyzed, because one cannot be sure that the superficial dominance of religion in terms of the political and cultural patterns of the past was real, and that art was at that time truly servile.[52] The paintings of Lescaux, the Hopi pottery, the historical paintings of a Ferdinand David, may hint that we should dig deeper and even farther back in time for the first enunciation of the aesthetic symbolic form. Here we may perceive the first thrust, the first creative distillation of art's own unique demands.

What is probably just as necessary is the concomitant awareness that the path upward to cultural progress can be as easily tilted downward into a pattern of dissolution. Cassirer came to grips with this problem only at the end of his career, in *The Myth of the State*. As Harry Slochower pointed out, the element of conflict in culture can act to destroy that which is unique about artistic freedom.[53] Indeed, merely because mankind has reached a point of philosophical awareness of the special nature of the aesthetic vision does not mean that all modern societies will uphold the inner integrity of the artistic. It may be, as Cassirer noted for language under the Nazis, that the superficial material expression of art — architecture, painting, music, literature — is furthered in that many individuals are thus fully engaged. But it could also be that the inner integrity and freedom of purpose that allow the aesthetic vision to flow freely from within the individual into a variety of social patterns is negated by political or commercial restraints. The aesthetic then must continually be on guard against, if not the suffocating embrace of myth, then the iron glove of political or economic coercion.

VIII *The Development of Art*

"Myth, language, and art," said Cassirer, "begin as a concrete, undivided unity which is only gradually resolved into a triad of independent modes of spiritual creativity."[54] Like language, the pictorial image must free itself from the mythic union with the concretely real. The sensuous reality of the word is abandoned for a representational function as it frees itself of the magicomythical modality. So, too, the aesthetic domain is created for the "image" only to the extent that it is perceived as a formulation and not a tangible reality.

Language must forego the richness and wealth of sensuous, concrete, and immediate experience to fulfill its representative symbolic function. Purely discursive communication has little of the original feelingness or expressive concreteness of the old mythical level. Language seen as a totality need not evolve as a whole toward the representative. The aesthetic domain may capture that element of immediacy and sensuosity that inheres in the original unity of expressive behavior. But, to do so, as language itself is freed to evolve in its logical function, the purely aesthetic dimension in language must be discovered by man. "This regeneration is achieved as language becomes an avenue of artistic expression," says Cassirer. "Here it recovers the fullness of life, but it is no longer a life mythically bound and fettered, but an aesthetically liberated life."[55]

What is achieved by language through poetry, especially lyric poetry, is achieved by each of the domains of art. Again, it must be emphasized that the transition to the aesthetic mode is not necessarily a historical event. More important, it represented to Cassirer a logical step forward and as such can happen at various times in history; it can even necessitate rediscovery over and over again.

The key to understanding the nature of the artistic is roughly parallel to that which helps us to interpret religion. The uniqueness of the religious domain, as it contrasts with the earlier expressive mythological states of awareness, is not the particular content of religion, whether it be polytheistic, personalistic, or monotheistic. It is rather our attitude toward the meaning of the symbols representative of divinity. Before, the symbol "signified something objectively real, the immediate work of God, a mystery." Now the religious is characterized by the meaning that is consciously attached to the symbol, a meaning that has new and richer intellective possibilities and one that will retain an always dynamic relationship to the symbol. The concrete symbols of religious feeling and meaning are necessary for each religion. The intelligible cannot completely cast off either the concrete or the sensuous. The concrete and sensuous, if they become overly real and tangible, lose their depths of symbolic meaning and become primitive mythic symbols; they will reflect a preconscious awareness of the divisions of experience, the sacred and the profane, mana and taboo: "the involvement and opposition of meaning and image are among the essential conditions of religion," Cassirer concludes.[56]

The special nature of art is evident at this point. For, in the art symbol, this dynamic tension between concrete imagery and intellectual meaning is effaced. The immediacy of the concrete object can be accepted as such. It is, however, not accepted as signifying a reality higher than its concreteness would imply. It is not a real God, a spirit, a totem. Nor is the image surmounted by a higher spiritual significance, a holy spirit, or an ethical imperative.

The image is accepted as a concrete symbol that represents only a pure sensuous immediacy. It is enjoyed for itself, as a consummatory object. Thus, a new attitude is here reflected in man, an attitude that was inherent in all earlier stages of symbolic expression, but one which needed to be freed of its servitude to extraneous intentional purposes. The aesthetic consciousness "gives itself to pure 'contemplation,' developing the form of vision in contrast to all forms of action, the images fashioned in this frame of consciousness gain for the first time a truly immanent significance. They confess themselves to be illusion as opposed to the empirical reality of things; but this illusion has its own truth because it possesses its own law. In the return to this law there arises a new freedom of consciousness: the image no longer reacts upon the spirit as an independent material thing but becomes for the spirit a pure expression of its own creative power."[57]

Man's discovery that all objects, sounds, motions, colors, can be infused with a special attitude, an independent symbolic modality, not restricted or reducible to mythic, religious, scientific, or representational approaches, was of revolutionary import for man. For, out of the purely perceptual concreteness of appreciation and meaning was reborn a structure for viewing experience.

IX   *Artistic Form*

It would be wrong to view the essence of art as located in the sensuous present, in that moment of aesthetic appreciation. One could argue that the aesthetic conciousness, to the extent that it can contemplate objects of nature or the artifacts of man in terms of their sensual qualities, has risen to a special plane of awareness. Thus, we are again looking at a development in man that may well have been facilitated by social and historical circumstances.

For Cassirer, searching for the causes in the development of the aesthetic consciousness was less important than tracing its inner structure as it exemplifies the phenomenology of thought. It is in the structure of aesthetic perception that this new level of consciousness is revealed. For man cannot merely contemplate and immerse himself in the sensual, the momentary, and the concrete. Thus, art in its surface character, its perceptual phenomena, serves also as a vehicle for the development of thought. Its own particular nature, however, allows it to develop the special modality of thought for human culture and makes it a symbolic form.

The uniqueness of art as contrasted with the other symbolic domains is reflected on by Cassirer as follows:

> Language and science are abbreviations of reality; art is an intensification of reality. Language and science depend upon one and the same process of abstraction; art may be described as a continuous process of concretion.... What science is searching for is some central feature of a given object from which all its particular qualities may be derived.... But art does not admit of the sort of conceptual simplification and deductive generalization. It does not inquire into the qualities or causes of things; it gives us the intuition of the form of things. But this too is by no means a mere repetition of something we had before. It is a true and genuine discovery. The artist is just as much a discoverer of the forms of nature as the scientist is a discoverer of facts or natural laws.[58]

This aspect of discovery is the key to understanding why art cannot be reduced to a sensory immersion in things. Man does not confront things as "they are." He infuses them with meaning. Thus, even in his common sense perception, man views the objects of experience in terms of their constant features in order to create a behavioral map of the world within which he must function. But, as Cassirer noted, aesthetic experience is much richer. Here, the world "is pregnant with infinite possibilities." But these possibilities do not inhere in the things themselves. The modality that we call the aesthetic transforms ordinary experience by finding in its sensory character a new set of formal principles, ordinarily hidden from the prosaic eye.

According to Cassirer, "To the extent that human language can express everything, the lowest and the highest things, art can embrace and pervade the whole sphere of human experience. Nothing in the physical or moral world, no natural thing and no human action, is by its nature and essence excluded from the realm of art, because nothing resists its formative and creative process."[59] Its ability to do this, to find artistic sense in "sensation," is rooted in the formal possibilities of the aesthetic as a symbolic form.

Where does this formal principle lie, from whence does it come, how does it develop, what are its inner logical principles? Certainly the power inheres in the structure of thought itself, the self-conscious ability of man to focus on experience in terms of the aesthetic attitude. And yet the material that we deal with — space, lines, sounds, colors — also determines or shapes the possibilities inherent in the aesthetic attitude. But at no two moments in history have these external conditions in reality limited the almost infinite possibilities for artistic transformation. Still, says Cassirer, we do note that discernible and enduring art forms have arisen, each encompassing a particular dimension of cultural experience:

> It is the structure, the balance and order, of those forms which affects us in the work of art. Every art has its own characteristic idiom, which is unmistakable and unexchangeable. The idioms of the various arts may be interconnected, as, for instance, when a lyric is set to music or a poem is illustrated; but they are not translatable into each other. Each idiom has a special task to fulfill in the 'architectonic' of art.[60]

The very concept of architectonics raises questions with regard to Cassirer's distinction between religion and art. Is art really freed from the tension with which religion is forced to live: between the object of religious feeling and its intellectual meaning? Is it true that art can join with an image in "pure contemplation?"[61] Is the distinction between sensory object and the "architechtonics of form" itself a tension out of which the dynamic evolution of art can be sprung? But artistic form, while a silent constraining principle, in that it does not connote theology or metaphysics in opposition to the concrete particularity of the aesthetic objects, certainly shapes and directs the individual things — musical notes, paint on canvas — toward a structure of meaning. The individual composition, painting, even dance step, in its particularity, is given power of meaning through its joining to the formal traditions of the art. As Cassirer puts it: "The beautiful is essentially and necessarily symbol because and insofar as it is split within itself, because it is always and everywhere both one and double. In this split, in the attachment to the sensuous, and in the rising above the sensuous, it not only expresses the tension which runs through our 'consciousness' — but reveals by this means the original and basic polarity of Being itself."[62]

X *Art As Creative Dynamic*

The tension that exists between material concreteness and formal
development is dynamic. In this interaction lie the possibilities for
creativity in art. Viewed from a symbolic perspective, art is a transformation of the surface sensual and material experiences of man
through the intermediary of the deepest resources in the human
psyche. The transformative powers of art achieve their most
condensive impact through specific formal structures.

Whenever art is recognized as such, there are established vehicles
within which materials and artifacts can be subject to this aesthetic
transformation. Thus, beautiful rock and metal are created into
jewelry, clay and vegetable colors are molded in pottery, even the
most prosaically functional tools seemingly are subject to aesthetic
transformations. Thus, a key element in the creation of high art is
the existence of forms having the expressive possibilities inherent in
this deeply rooted potentiality of man.

In all his writings that touch on art, Cassirer returned again and
again to the lyric poem. The lyric was the epitome of the aesthetic
form of language. Here, language departed from its representative,
descriptive function and entered into a new relationship with man.
The lyric poem is the refined and distilled embodiment of that sense
of emotional power, awareness of the depths of feeling as it objectifies itself in metaphorical transformation. It is language and it is
art. Feeling and form are joined to tangible sounds to create a new
objective awareness that never existed before, says Cassirer:

> The lyric is no mere intensification or sublimation of an exclamation. It
> is no mere divulging of a momentary mood nor does it seek simply to tra-
> verse the scale of tones between extremes of emotion, between sorrow and
> joy, pain and pleasure, serenity and despair. If the lyric poet succeeds in
> giving "melody and voice" to pain, by so doing, he has not only enveloped
> it in a new covering; he has changed its inner nature. Through the medium
> of the emotions he has enabled us to glimpse spiritual depths which until
> now were closed and inaccessible to himself as well as to us.... He shows
> us life and reality in a form in which we feel we have never known it before
> ... discloses to us a *knowledge* which cannot be grasped in abstract con-
> cepts which stands before us, nevertheless, as the revelation of something
> new, something never before known or familiar. As its greatest achieve-
> ment, we owe to art the fact that in its particulars it allows us to feel and to
> know what is objective; that it places all its objective creations before us
> with a concreteness and individuality which floods them with a life of
> strength and intensity.[63]

We can thus understand why certain forms of art rank higher in terms of their aesthetic possibilities. Their very material components allow of a much more radical inner transformation than other forms. The limitations inherrent in jewelry, perfumes, and other more decorative arts are due to their limited possibilities for objectification. Also, to the extent that an art form is relatively "indifferent," in that it cannot prosper as much from the individual mark of the creative artist, it is also limited. "The artist's eye is not simply an eye that reacts to or reproduces sense impressions. Its activity is not confined to receiving or registering the impressions of outward things or combining these impressions in new and arbitrary ways. A great painter or musician is not characterized by his sensitiveness to color or sounds but by his power to elicit from his static material a dynamic life of forms. Only in this sense then, can the pleasure we find in art be objectified."[64]

The great arts — music, painting, poetry, and literature — have the capacity to allow for an almost infinite plasticity of expression. The creative artist here has a material — language, sound, paint — that can be processed and reprocessed into new structural modes of expression. Those great ages of art have been eras when cultural conditions combined with the availability of forms — the lyric poem, the novel, the sonata form, the violin, oil paint, canvas, and perspective, bronze or marble, the arch and the flying buttress — and allowed artists to plumb that boundless reservoir of dynamic meanings from which art is created.

But, what is important is not the mere expression of this emotional reservoir of dynamic perceptions. It is that the artist have the capacity to utilize his powers of empathy and awareness to recreate the existing forms, to find new possibilities in the given, even to the extent of carrying forth a great revolution or reshaping a basic art form into a wholly new mode of expression. There is a kind of knowledge here, universal, yet so personal. Unlike science, which deals with the universal dimensions of the material world and objectifies this inherent universality in laws and principles that all mankind can know, the artist's universality is a more individual kind; it is a unique vision of the formal relationships of man and nature. The rhythms, patterns, images of the arts in their own way constitute a multitude of insights into both the dynamic of life and the structural underpinnings that make its unities and diversities possible. But the language of art is both unique in that it is "aesthetic form," and diverse in that there are many possibile ways that this form can be embodied, and many types and degrees of revelation that the creative symbolic powers of man can engage.

XI *Creativity and Freedom*

Cassirer devoted relatively little systematic attention to art as such. References to poetry and the aesthetic dimensions of language, a chapter on art in *An Essay on Man,* as well as a number of studies of artistic personalities in the cultural history of the West represent his work here. There can be no doubt that it ranked high in his analysis of culture, in his estimation of its import for symbolic thought. Compared to the sciences and even myth and religion, it was a far too intangible area, and Cassirer evidently could not fathom its inner meaning as it revealed itself in the evolution of Western civilization. Religious, scientific, and philosophical ideas enunciated themselves clearly. Art was garbed in its multifarious concrete objects and experiences.

His deep commitment to the pursuit of the structure of scientific ideas dominated his concern with the structure of knowledge. Art presented such rapid historical advances that even the powerful thrust for universal envisagement seen in scientific knowledge could not match. There was in art that almost magical fluidity and freedom of expression, the utilization of the material object, the sensuous moment, as a means of opening up to the world the most secret sources of the human imagination. What came so easily and necessarily from the symbolic form of art was extracted with such difficulty from science. Art, liberated of cultural obstacles, always found ways, legitimate or subversive, to objectify itself. The scientific imagination had much more difficulty in making itself felt. Where art dodged, infiltrated, transmuted itself into new appearances, the creative scientist seemingly needed to push over the existing edifice.

As Harry Slochower has pointed out, it is here that a most subtle interpretation of freedom enters into a relationship with art.[65] For human freedom is fulfilled in that most typical human function, the symbolic act. The symbolic act is a creative act, an organization out of any concatenation of perceptual materials or experiences into a synthesis of meaning. Human culture in its variety and historic process is an exemplification of the recreation of experience through the symbolic medium.

Art is the purest and most direct symbolic ordering of those deeply rooted imaginative powers that lie at the source of man's symbolic disposition. The meaning of the aesthetic experience lies in its consummatory experiencing. The formal elements are always immanent in each aesthetic object and experience. One does not have to go to a dictionary to understand the import of a Renoir painting, a sonnet by Donne, or a Mozart quartet.

If human freedom is fulfilled in giving man as much leave to mine the possibilities of symbolic recreation, then art is the paradigmatic symbolic form. It needs no intermediaries, it is the living stuff of culture. The universal passion for art can be understood by this fact, that no material is immune to aesthetic transformation. The modes, gradations, directions of artistic creativity are infinite at every step in time. The test of the impact and power of art lies in its utilization and reconstruction of the given formal element in the esthetic context of any period. But given a powerful enough personality, an imagination endowed with the capacity to objectify these capabilities, new aesthetic forms can be created.

One wishes that Cassirer had explored this dimension of freedom in greater historical detail. For with the enormous challenges to the symbolic integrity of the high culture of the West in our contemporary era, as well as those challenges in other periods of history, one wonders whether the debasement of art does constitute the first step in the emasculation of freedom. The question thus remains, as we perceive the advances in art from the standpoint of history and the gradual ennobling power of the artist, how do we discern the gradual corruption and the turning of the artist's high purposes into forms of expression that interdict the freedom and intentionality of the aesthetic?

XII *History*

Cassirer was himself one of the great intellectual historians of the twentieth century. His entire orientation as a philosopher — and this includes his systematic works such as *The Philosophy of Symbolic Forms* — is permeated by a sensitivity to the relevance of the historical tradition and the context of ideas. And finally, one of the great volumes on the philosophy of history, entitled *Philosophy and History: The Ernst Cassirer Festschrift* (1936), was dedicated to him on the occasion of his sixtieth birthday. The contributors include the greatest historical minds of our time.

All this is prelude to saying that prior to *An Essay on Man* (1944) Cassirer did not consider history as a symbolic form. Yet, in this book, its placement is after myth and religion, language, art, and before science. The placement is important because it reflects Cassirer's more mature consideration of this symbolic form from the standpoint of his subsequent concerns and from having had time to reflect on the larger significance of his earlier work.

Several aspects of this inclusion and placement of history are significant. One is that there is a clear cut developmental hierarchy in the symbolic forms. Now, for example, myth and religion are placed before language, in contrast to their treatment in *The Philosophy of Symbolic Forms,* where the volume on language preceded that dealing with myth. History is thus seen as a less rigorous or discursive form of knowledge than the physical sciences. And, in the treatment of history, as we shall note, this distinction is kept and analyzed in more detail.

The second aspect is related to the fact that Cassirer noted a significant difference in the modality of thought between physical science and history. In his *The Problem of Knowledge,* Volume 4 (completed in 1940), he had brought his study of the problem of knowledge from the Renaissance to completion. The four volumes of *Das Erkenntnisproblem* gave him a final perspective from the standpoint of the new post-Hegelian biological sciences as well as an opportunity to study in detail the burst of historical writing and the discussions of the philosophy of history up through the first third of the twentieth century.

In a sense, what this study had brought forward to Cassirer was the realization that a basic, if immanent, tenet espoused in *The Philosophy of Symbolic Forms* had been fulfilled, almost within his lifetime. This is the emergence of a new modality of thought, self-conscious about its canons of logic, evidence, subject matter, and predictive status. The study of history as well as the vast increase in historical writings showed clearly that history was a unique and independent dimension of human thought. That it came so late in the development of knowledge again confirms that process of cultural distillation by which the human mind is gradually freed of its unself-conscious immersion in the given of culture, to reflect on its various intentional symbolic powers, and then stimulated to mine and exploit these powers.

Thus, as we have noted with regard to myth and language, the distillation of the enormous emotional forces reflective of the expressive stage of symbolic thought was a prelude for the development of religion, art, philosophy, and then science. Only then could philosophy, the sciences, and the arts in turn precipitate out their various component disciplines and fields of endeavor. As Cassirer pointed out, the first self-conscious awareness of history as a modality of rational analysis was given to us by the Athenian, Thucydides. But it was not until fairly recent times that a debate over the nature of historical study so enlarged the intellectual context of discussion that we could, as Cassirer did, separate history from the general structure of knowledge and label it a distinct symbolic form.

It took both the detailed analysis of the structure of physics, matehmatics, and biology, as well as history, declares Cassirer, to make it clear that what was evident in history was not merely another scientific discipline with different materials but a wholly new mode of analysis made necessary by the utterly unique vision:

> The historian, like the physicist, lives in a material world. Yet what he finds at the very beginning of his research is not a world of physical objects but a symbolic universe — a world of symbols. He must, first of all, learn to read these symbols. Any historical fact, however simple it may appear, can only be determined and understood by such a previous analysis of symbols. Not things or events but documents or monuments are the first and immediate objects of our historical knowledge. Only through the mediation and intervention of these symbolic data can we grasp the real historical data — the events and the men of the past.[66]

There is in this statement more than an assertion of history's unique symbolic materials. Throughout Cassirer's chapter on history in *An Essay On Man* is the recognition of the purely symbolic character of all scientific knowledge. The manner in which this spectrum of knowledge draws in a general vision of human culture serves to emphasize the creative and constructive character of historical research and to place in the background overstated attempts to reconstruct history with strict objectivity, in the spirit of nineteenth-century ideals.

Here, as in other symbolic forms, one would expect to find an underlying logical principle, whether it is the sense of deeply veiled human emotions, as in myth or religion, or the quest for perceptual meaning as expressed in pure form, as in art, or the larger universal

logical assertions that we find in the sciences. Cassirer did find this
quest for universality in history as he did in the other rational dis-
ciples. "'Universality' is not a term which designates a certain field
of thought; it is an expression of the very character, of the function
of thought. Thought is always universal," declares Cassirer.[67] He
goes on to say:

> In his quest of truth the historian is bound to the same formal rules as
> the scientist. In his modes of reasoning and arguing, in his inductive infer-
> ences, in his investigation of causes, he obeys the same general laws of
> thought as a physicist or biologist. So far as these fundamental theoretical
> activities of the human mind are concerned we can make no discrimination
> between the different fields of knowledge.... Historical and scientific
> thought are distinguished not by their logical form but by their objectives
> and subject matter.... History does not aim to disclose a former state of
> the physical world but rather a former stage of human life and human cul-
> ture.... What we call the historic sense does not change the shape of
> things, nor does it detect in them a new quality. But it does give to things
> and events a new depth.... What the historian is in search of is rather the
> materialization of the spirit of a former age.[68]

Cassirer did not raise the issue of the one or the many in historical research. Is there a plurality of equally acceptable interpretations of the symbols of the past? How are we to judge or to guide
ourselves for the present in the light of conflicting approaches and
criteria of historical research? And, given methodological agreement, how can we decide between different interpretations of accepted historical data? For Cassirer did recognize the ultimate re-
creative character of history. The truths of history cannot be fairly
tested in the crucible of today's events.

The words and phrases that emerge from his treatment reflect his
basic sense of indecision: "a knowledge of ourselves," "an act of
the productive imagination," "historical knowledge is a branch of
semantics," "history strives after an 'objective anthropormor-
phism," "in order to possess the world of culture we must inces-
santly reconquer it by historical recollection. But recollection does
not mean merely the act of reproduction. It is a new intellectual
synthesis — a constructive act."

And finally, he concludes: "Art and history are the most powerful instruments of our inquiry into human nature.... History as
well as poetry is an organon of our self-knowledge, an indis-

pensable instrument for building up our human universe.... Life in the light of history remains a great realistic drama, with all its tensions and conflicts, its greatness and misery, its hopes and illusions, its displays of energies and passions."[69]

Thus, there is an essential mystery to the inner meaning of our historical reconstructions, and creative reconstructions they are. Unlike the physical sciences, where the temporally neutral character of material experience is subject to never-ending refinement and is always leading toward a universal pattern of acceptance, history must be constantly rediscovered, its new meaning for each successive age carved out as much from the demotic myths of the contemporary age as from more philosophical perspectives on the human condition. The great theoretical reconstruction of physical science can be tested easily; it can be accepted or rejected by all mankind. The historical vision is a product of the prevailing cultural ethos similar to those canons of aesthetic reputability. The facts, documents, and artifacts are the pivots of the discipline of history.

History inhabits that intermediate area between art and science. As Cassirer intuited, the materials of art and history are the grist for their respective subject matters. But art is freer from that point on. The form of art is ineffable; it is an inner discipline, a tacit pillar of culture. History is determined by the more concrete intellectual demands of its age, to reconstruct its materials in accordance with a given logical order. The creative powers of the historian are enclosed in more concrete requirements. But here, too, the "facts" and the intellectual requirements of the day are merely challenges for meanings that will establish a new order of ideas. Fustel de Coulanges, for example, in his *La Cité Antique* (*The Ancient City*), (1864) — in spite of conflicting interpretations — still inspired a whole new category of historical research into the origin of religious practices. It then produced a new order of historical "facts."[70]

That history constitutes another organon of man's self-knowledge opens up the possibility that we can uncover and explore other existing or incipient symbolic forms. Is there a psychological explanation that could distill the varying intentional attitudes from whence these symbolic forms come? Is there a logical structure relating these various forms to each other? Cassirer did not have time to answer these and other puzzling questions.

XIII   The Philosophy of Symbolic Forms *in Perspective*

The conception of *The Philosophy of Symbolic Forms* represents the second phase of Cassirer's philosophical development. It owes its conception and direction to the culminating researches into the history of scientific knowledge that dominated his attention up until World War I. The conclusions here reached with regard to the nature of scientific knowledge raised questions congruent with what Cassirer believed he had achieved in extending the Marburg conception of science. He felt these issues to be of potentially revolutionary importance for our understanding of knowledge.

To see the relationship between the two stages of his development, we should reiterate here the basic philosophical and scientific perspectives of Cassirer's Marburg Kantianism. Dominating our view of knowledge is the import of the concept that we search for sense in sensation. We do not confront "reality" directly; we confront it through the intermediary of conceptual interpretation. "External reality" is a conception not useful in our description of the knowledge we have through experience. Nor can we reduce experience to any particular and simple elements. Experience is never raw; it is always formed. Rational man's search is for the principles by which we can understand this process of synthesis.

The laws of science in their advance in complexity and in the reach toward intellectual control of nature are not objective in terms of revealing an unvarying view of nature. Even as they pivot from one *a priori* standpoint to another, they show at once the role that basic experiential materials interacting with conceptual elements play in this advance. Scientific laws are conceptual tools for integrating experience. New theories become necessary because the old principles find certain experiential elements indigestible. The theories of science are convenient, functional; they refer to no ultimate entities. They are merely rules for fostering further inquiries.

Two principles seem to be at work in the evolution of science. One is the continuing search in thought for laws that encompass more universal aspects of our experience. We search for universal principles through rational inquiry. At the same time, the character of the theories we utilize undergoes a parallel evolution. The theories evolve from sensuous or substantive concepts that mirror things and sensations to more functional, ideal, or abstract relational theories. The road toward the universal in science is seemingly traversed through increasingly abstract, ideal symbolic referents.

The thought occurred to Cassirer that since science is a modality of thought, a way of looking at experience, then the intractability of other dimensions of culture to the canons of science may be due less to their purported inherent irrationality than to the fact that science, language, art, and religion have carved out different symbolic domains reflecting differing human interests and needs. Until one could put science in its proper role, not as an all-encompassing objective revelation of the universe subjecting all human experience to one established "rule of the game," but merely as one important organon of man's search for symbolic meaning, a general understanding of knowledge could not be obtained.

Cassirer's work on Einstein's relativity theory confirmed his expectations about the functional purposes and claims of this particular scientific revolution and set him on his journey to find new forms of sense in areas of "sensory" experience quite different from those that preoccupied the physical sciences, mathematics, and logic. The shift is thus from a conception of knowledge with a capital "K" to the problem of the structure of the various forms of knowing. Immediately implied is the broader perspective of culture theory. The forms of discursive knowing — science and mathematics — are not, as they are in the modern physicalist traditions, the paradigm of all human thought.[71] They are merely functional tools for but one kind of intellectual activity.

The symbolic-form concept thus implies cultural parity in our understanding of the diverse manifestations of cultural thought. Cassirer set himself the task of uncovering the various structures of thought, distinct from the logical. He also attempted to delineate the inner pattern of law unique to each symbolic form. His approach was certainly Kantian in the use of the constants space, time, and number as comparative prisms through which he could develop his analysis of language and myth. But, at the same time, he searched carefully among the various authorities on whom he relied. He wanted to develop his theory so as to allow the ethnological, historical, and systematic studies to speak in their own contexts and not be quickly subsumed under models appropriate to other disciplines or other existing philosophical positions.

The result was to establish the unique modalities of symbolic expression and of creativity on myth, religion, commonsense language, art, and history. Underlying their discreteness as forms of cultural expression lies an assumption of diversity based on a fundamental difference in human attitude or intentionality by which perceptual experience is focused in one direction — art — rather than in another — science. Cassirer had less to say about this inner principle of differentiation. He may have been dealing here with a fundamental psychological disposition. His interest, however, was in principles and in the outward expression of these principles in the structures of forms of activity. The human awareness of power or of the forces for good or evil in myth, the immersion in both form and concreteness that exhausted the perceptual moment in art — these were only summary comments beyond which Cassirer was afraid to go. To try to explain further would be to deal with hypothetical inner constructs, perhaps to be forced to reify internal principles into metaphysical entities.

The logic of art is irreducible to that of science. The rational use of political language ought not to be degenerated to its mythical exploitation. These are ways of understanding the autonomies of thought in producing the variegated life of culture. But this understanding is paralleled by another important dimension in the symbolic forms. This dimension involves the progressive evolution of cultural thought as exemplified in the historic extrusion of unique structures of symbolic expression along a variety of intentional pathways. In the earliest unities of expressive experience thought holds linguistic, mythic, and aesthetic elements in a unity; symbol is yet joined to concrete reality — meaning is absorbed into the object — and words become realities. Thence there is a gradual precipitation of the more specialized patterns of thought. From this early — and theoretical — unity, myth evolves into religious forms having clearly articulated dogmatic, ethical, and ritual patterns alongside earlier mythological traditions; language is enabled to evolve in grammar and syntax so that consistent logical relationships can be more easily articulated through structural simplicity; the arts evolve in terms of their own dynamic principles, the purely aesthetic intuitions being freed from practical sociopolitical demands as well as those of religious or mythical persuasion. If art is to be joined with other cultural valences, as in a cathedral or as in song or opera, the integrity of each is still maintained in a unity of function.

This constitutes a rather mysterious process of development

about which Cassirer himself was hesitant to hypothesize. Certainly, the freeing of each mode of cultural discourse is partially a product of general cultural development. But within each of these evolutionary developments, there seems to be an inner dynamic that in its own particular way parallels that found in science. An inner purificalion in art and religion directs each toward more universal qualities in its formal organization.

Great art and great religious thought, though they evolve from particular cultural and historical matrices, yet speak to mankind with universal power. This universality of appeal is buttressed by the freeing of each form of the limitations provided by or rooted in the materiality out of which it grows. Whether they be words, or paint, or stone, or mathematical symbols, the greatest symbolic creations exploit the ideational elements, the patterns, structure, or models from which the specific embodiment takes on its own unique shape. Form becomes the means by which thought works its creative and imaginative transmutation of the given of cultural experience. Thus, in religion, in the arts, in science, philosophy, or logic, the claim of significant creative work is always embodied in the fact of the triumph of form or concept over the limitations inherent in the specificity of the concrete materials utilized.

CHAPTER 5

Thought and Human Nature

I *Intuitive Understanding*

IN postulating the dialectical development of language and myth out of and beyond the purely expressive phase of human experience to a point where more permanent and stable configurations of experience are ordered for thought and behavior, Cassirer was opening up a perplexing issue. He did not necessarily subscribe to the idea that mythic thought involved a unidirectional phase in the history of man. It was a logical category that was supported by empirical evidence in anthropology and the psychology of human development. It was the root stage that led to the great intellectual threshold of commonsense language that subsequently opened up for man those important symbolic realms of higher thought — religion, literature, philosophy, and science.

The problem lay in explaining how this inner tendency toward the secular stability of thought and language developed out of mythic expressivity. What gave dynamic to this dialectical transformation, this inner tendency that seemed able to draw out stable configurations of belief and action from the frenzied, fearful, fluid world of mythic expression?

In short, what was it that allowed myth to be so uniquely primitive — denied the principles of ideality and universality that found increasingly purified exemplification in the higher cultural symbolic forms? Where could we root ideality and universality if they were only immanent in that primal stratum of mythic thought? Certainly, unless one faced these issues, the door would be opened to a host of philosophical, if not metaphysical, misinterpretations. Even a logically conceived developmental view of cultural thought must embody a principle by which we can understand the transformation such as occurred from myth to religion. If not an efficient cause, then we needed at least a formal cause.

Cassirer was aware of these problems, even while he was completing the first two volumes of *The Philosophy of Symbolic Forms*. In a sense, deeper theoretical roots were needed to hold the various symbolic forms in context. It was not enough to note the expressive, emotional function as logically primitive. Further, it could not be that all of man's existence at this level of cultural life could be exhaustingly permeated by emotional elements. The mere contrast between those basic mythic elements — the sacred and profane — implied some breathing space, the existence of a relatively restful, prosaic secular dimension. So, too, with language. If, indeed, sensuous elements dominated, the existence here of large vocabularies seemingly reflected the particularity and the practicality of sensory experience.

This condition did not of course rule out the existence of formal elements, grammars, syntax, phonologies. Cassirer stated,

> . . . in our analysis of language we have striven to differentiate three strata, which we termed the phases of sensuous, intuitive, and purely conceptual expression. This classification was not meant historically — as though we supposed that in the development of language we could single out successive stages, one embodying the purely sensuous type, the others the purely intuitive or conceptual type. That would be an absurdity, if only because the total phenomenon of language is first constituted by the whole of its structural elements, so that this whole must be regarded as present in the most primitive as well as the most highly developed language.[1]

Thus, at the very least, the dialectic, which propelled thought forward into more fully articulated symbolic modes as well as more ideational and universal exemplifications in culture, had for itself both a thesis and an antithesis. The antithesis must be myth and the expressive attitude. For the root stock — the thesis — out of which the crowning glory of culture will one day develop must be situated in some basic logical form, if not its concrete replication. The thesis must be embodied in ordinary secular experience; and it was in this context of his search for an understanding of this postulation that a variety of intellectual stimuli gradually led Cassirer to a realization that the primitivity of myth, its placement as expressive form, was thus logical and not in any sense historical. He had not yet, in the mid-1920s, to face the concreteness of this truth in the mythologies of fascism. By the time he wrote *The Myth of the State,* he was well prepared.

When one reads the third volume of *The Philosophy of Symbolic Forms,* it is almost as if an inner debate is therein being rehearsed as Cassirer sought for an understanding of this issue. We see two sets of influences, each powerful and persuasive, and yet each leading off in a different direction. The first reflected the newly developing phenomenological and existential movements of Husserl and Heidegger, supported as they were by Nicolai Hartmann, a student of Natorp who had subsequently moved into phenomenology. There did exist this tendency in Natorp's analysis of subjective experience. Cassirer was not only sensitive to the ideas of this group, but respectful of both Natorp's intellectual concerns and the reasons for which a thinker might therefore move more directly out of the Kantian perspective. The work of Henri Bergson was also at this time influential in redirecting concern for the more dynamic and internal sources of human experience.

The second element seems, at least to this reader, to be a more typical Cassirer fascination. This was with the writings of Karl Büehler, Clara and Wilhelm Stern, Wolfgang Köhler, Ewald Hering, and David Katz, all philosophically oriented experimental psychologists. The decisive influence probably came through the aegis of Cassirer's brother-in-law, Kurt Goldstein, who was working at this time with Adhemar Gelb in the Frankfurt Neurological Institute, and was especially interested in the various perceptual and cognitive pathologies that had been induced in brain-wounded veterans of World War I. As Cassirer noted, it was the writings of Henry Head, at first in various periodicals, and then, in 1926, in his classic two-volume work, *Aphasia and Kindred Disorders of Speech,* that stimulated this interest.[2]

First, we had a deep philosophical concern for the nature of ordinary commonsense experience as expressed by Bergson, and the phenomenological existentialists. Added to this were the researches by cognitively oriented experimental psychologists, broadening the context of traditional psychological research to animals, children, human color perception, and holistic perceptual configurations in the mind. For our Marburg Kantian these latter studies constituted a small but clarifyingly decisive shift in orientation. He now saw that it is the basic perceptual act of intuiting experience, an act that takes place in an almost unself-conscious and spontaneous manner, that constitutes that basic and decisive productive level of symbolic thought out of which all more self-conscious and specialized symbolic functioning evolves.

It is typical of Cassirer's methodology that in attempting to work through the problem of the unitary substrate for symbolic thought, he posed issues extracted from the current philosophical literature and confronted it critically with evidence taken from the most contemporary scientific circles. Thus, the phenomenological concern to see intuitive experience directly and wholly and not to fall into empiricistic or rationalistic bifurcations and dualisms is shown to involve its own particular antinomies, whether they be Hartmann's body and soul or Husserl's primary content and the intentional, or the material and the noetic. These constructs all retain dualistic elements.[3]

But the psychologists now seemed to indicate another trend. The direct confrontation of the self with the world is not a "pure" involvement that contrasts to the more abstract intentional evaluation of experience of the Kantians. Evaluation is in itself a primary occurrence. Experience consists of organized wholes, whether they be gestalts of faces, or whether they be ordered sequences of colors. Experience, even as it is shaped out of the child's confrontation with the world, is always an interpreted intuition first and directly, and not a secondary residual product that one renders after immersing oneself in the wholeness of the world. These were the views of contemporary psychological thought.

Cassirer followed somewhat the same line of argumentation, supporting his protagonists, that he took with regard to the problem of the status of scientific theory. Is theory reducible to sensory experience or is our view of sensation itself a derived concept? In the present context of intuitive experience, one is forced to argue from similar grounds. What we have discovered with regard to scientific laws, that they are conventionally organized conceptual tools to provide a map for future experimentation and thought, is paralleled in ordinary life. Where scientific laws are consciously organized from the structure of theory and experiment, and thus highly abstracted from ordinary experience, the intuition of the world that is given to use as primary experience is likewise an organized structure of causes and effects, things and attributes, objects in space and time. Our abstractions from experience subsequently create such concepts as sensation, flow of experience, unitary wholeness.

Cassirer was now claiming that the very primordial mental act of the human being — the intuition of living experience — constituted an act of representation, of symbolic meaning. On this basic level of living and functioning, thought acted for man in the same general manner as it did on the various abstracted levels of cognition. Only in myth, science, and art, for example, the basic intuitive experience was enriched by reflecting varying intentional attitudes as well as significantly expanded domains of symbolic meaning.

The expression Cassirer gave to this level of intuitive representation, the original thesis of the dialectical progression of thought, was "symbolic pregnance":

> By symbolic pregnance we mean the way a perception as a sensory experience contains at the same time a certain non-intuitive meaning which it immediately and concretely represents. Here we are not dealing with base perceptive data, in which some sort of apperceptive acts are later grafted, through which they are interpreted, judged, transformed.... We determine the single thing in respect to its objective meaning, by articulating it with the spatio-temporal order, the causal order, and the order of thing and property. Through this ordering it takes on a specific directional meaning — a vector as it were, pointing to a determinate goal.... No conscious perception is merely given, a mere datum, which need only be mirrored; rather, every perception embraces a definite "character of direction" by which it points beyond its here and now.... We have everywhere seen that this kind of pregnance is distinguished by unmistakable characteristics from any purely quantitative accumulation or associative combination of perceptive images, and that it cannot be explained by reduction to purely discursive acts of judgment and inference. The symbolic process is like a single stream of life and thought which flows through consciousness, and which by this flowing movement produces the diversity and cohesion, the richness, the continuity, and constancy, of consciousness.[4]

Cassirer wanted to make several important points in this discussion. The perceptual act itself contains an "immanent organization." No "quantitative accumulation" of perceptions or series of associative combinations, typically empiricistic constructs, can bring forth the organization inherent in the symbolic intuitive act. Nor can purely logical or discursive acts of judgment or inferences, acts which imply something to be evaluated or analyzed, explain the inherent organization in the act of symbolization. At least on the intuitive level of experience the representational act is immediate. But it is not isolated. Cassirer cited Natorp's *Allgemeine Psychologie* (*General Psychology*) with approval, noting the rich relational character of perceptive experience, a relational richness which we can only appreciate after the fact by the use of more discursive forms of analysis.

Perhaps our difficulty in appreciating the immediacy, the pure relation, "a genuine a priori, an essentially first factor ... the true pulse of consciousness, whose secret is precisely that every beat strikes a thousand connections,"[5] is because the human being is so complicated that the most mundane perceptual experiences are interpenetrated by a vast variety of emotional, judgmental, anticipatory, and action modalities, a vast spider work of perspectives and complex structures of meanings. What is added to our representations on the intuitive level are varieties of aesthetic, social, and practical considerations that are culturally determined at a farther removed stage of learning. Cassirer was arguing that the intuitive level of symbolic thought, could we uncover it by peeling away social and cultural factors, constitutes a level of symbolic representation that must be universal to man.

II *Language and Aphasia*

In the context of ordinary life there is no clear separation of the intuitive representation of experience as it stems from perception as against the representational functions performed by language. Language and perception are stems of thought united in an "inner bond." Again, "the first universal is only guaranteed by the fact that it finds a hold and a firm precipitate in language."[6] And, of course, while we can observe that the infant, in response to external stimuli, responds in terms of objects and causes, and in a sense represents intuitive experience in terms of coherent meaning structures that guide its gradually maturing behavior, it is language that takes thought more completely on to its journey into abstraction.

Language and thought are thus intertwined to the point that it is extremely difficult to conceive of one without the other. Cassirer's discovery of the work of Henry Head and Kurt Goldstein was therefore a unique opportunity to understand the nature of the unity of symbolic thought, its various components and significance, as well as to see thought here in process of disintegration. Aphasia, by definition, constitutes a class of disabilities involving linguistic functions. Usually, these disfunctions are organic in nature, caused by injury or disease and thus traceable to some fairly specific areas of the brain as primary cause. The complexity of the brain and the variety of lesions and insults possible give rise to a diverse number of identifiable disabilities, apraxia and agnosia being, in addition to the more usual language disturbance in aphasia, related motor and optic disabilities.

The various attempts to understand aphasia in order to treat it resulted, for most of the nineteenth century, in a diagnosis that corresponded to the dominant sensationalist view of mental operations. Thus, Wernicke, as late as 1874 (in his *Manual of Brain Disorders*), would attempt to localize sound images in one part of the brain, motor images in another; in general, he attempted to establish that sense impressions had their specific physical substrate in the brain.[7] The world of experience grew up out of the capacity of the brain — in typical Berkeleyan and Humean models — to compare and associate given images and sense impressions with new ones that imprinted themselves on the brain and released the concrete neurological message.

Henry Head, who led the way toward the modern theoretical reintegration of these brain disorders, followed the work of Hughlings Jackson, who, from 1860–1890, had carved out a different conception of the problem. Jackson, an experimentalist and a member of the group of thinkers which included T. H. Huxley and Herbert Spencer, helped keep England at the forefront of scientific research. But, in Jackson's case, his strongly independent aspect of mind prevented him from being seduced by the older English empiricist model, a seduction to which his continental counterparts were not immune.

Instead of analyzing the speech losses of aphasics in terms of the discrete elements — letters and words — Jackson noted that the fundamental unit of impairment was the sentence. A word lost one day could reappear the next, whereas certain kinds of sentences seemed to be permanently affected. Jackson concluded that certain kinds of sentences were the key to understanding the specifics of the loss of language use. Thus, aphasics using language in emotional utterances, in interjectional ways, suffered less than when they attempted propositional or expository sentences. In the one, in which inner emotional states are expressed, there is little loss; in the other, where objective intentions are designated, there is profound disability. According to Jackson, "Loss of speech is, therefore, the loss of the power to propositionize. It is not only loss of power to propositionize aloud (to talk), but to propositionize either internally or externally, and it may exist when the patient remains able to utter some few words."[8]

By the time Head was assembling the accumulated body of research that related to aphasic and other disfunctions, he could generalize both with regard to speech defects and to a wide variety of behavioral malfunctions. At the very time that Cassirer had been extending his view of the symbolic status of scientific knowledge to the wider cultural domain, Head was likewise generalizing with regard to the basic structure of human behavior. The common root deficiency of such disorders of speech and action was an incapacity for symbolic behavior. According to Head, in the aphasic, ". . . any act of mental expression, which demands symbolic formulation, tends to be defective and the higher its propositional value the greater difficulty will it present. . . . Any modification of the task, which lessens the necessity for symbolic representation, will render its performance easier."[9]

The interesting, if bizarre, aspect of these pathologies was that they seemed not only to transcend the language-behavior dichotomy but to be an independent aspect of each modality. Thus, the breakdown of the symbolic attitude could be seen in purely verbal behavior with perception and motor activities remaining normal; or indeed, this relationship could be reversed. Regardless of the behavioral function that was affected, the common root was the inability of the person to act in the abstract, categorical, objectivizing modality.

Thus, an individual was unable to name generic colors or, in turn, to relate shades of colors, reds, or blues. But usually, if shown a specific object such as a strawberry, the word "red" appeared in the description, or was recognized perceptually in the act of separating the color "red" from various other colors. Both in the Frankfurt Neurological Institute, where Gelb and Goldstein worked, and in the Barmbecker Hospital in Hamburg, where Heinrich Embden introduced him to a number of special cases, Cassirer could appreciate the empirical evidence for this unique revocation of the symbolic attitude. Just as for Freud the breakdown of mental function gave him deep universal insights into the structure of the psyche, so too, in these aphasic imbalances in structure and function, Cassirer could understand better what had been so elusive a problem in understanding the psychological processes underlying the building up of the epistemological structure of experience and knowledge.

It was not merely a higher and lower stratum of thought, as Jackson originally hypothesized, that seemed to be revealed by the aphasic. Nor was it a matter of a split between the emotional and the representational, an element that Cassirer was wont to emphasize, again contrasting mythic expressivity with secular representation. In many cases, it was a matter of the patient being fixed to the prosaic and secular response to stimuli (always the concrete response, the particular behavioral need) that set off positive use, which under most circumstances seemed to be frozen. When color names could not be evoked, then sky or dead for blue or black could be elicited in response to stimuli. Somehow, a vague sense of generality was still intact, yet the universal linguistic term was not available. At other times, as in tactile aphasia, a patient could practically distinguish if a thing were hard, rough, or cold. But he could not identify a rock, a piece of sandpaper, or a coin. Sometimes, the thing was recognized as an object when held in one hand, but not when held in the other.

Gelb and Goldstein described the breakdown as a shift from the categorical attitude to the practical. This was especially emphasized in name amnesia. It was not a matter of a specific language defect. What had been lost was an attitude of mind, they concluded: "The categorical attitude and the possessions of language in its significatory function are expressions of one and the same basic attitude. Presumably neither of the two is cause or effect. It seems to us that the disturbance which gives rise to all the symptoms we find in our patients consists in an impairment of this fundamental attitude and a corresponding lapse into a more primitive attitude."[10]

What is not answered is the more difficult question as to whether disabilities in language such as these bar the way to higher forms of thought, logic, and mathematics, or even music, in that the loss here of the categorical attitude is considered a global loss for all subsequent mental possibilities. Because of the important role of language in the development of abstract intellectual powers, is this amnesic loss of language potentially short circuiting for thought?

A fascinating and perplexing example of the symbolic autonomy of intuitive forms of representation — linguistic and perceptual — as distinct from more complex, logical, and discursive kinds of thinking, is that of the German soldier, formerly a miner, who had been shot in the head. After his wound had healed, it was discovered that all that he could see were colored spots; he could dis-

tinguish the general height or breadth of things but could not identify concrete shapes, squares, lines, or curves.

But he adjusted and learned to recognize pictures and everyday
objects on the basis of this scanty information; he could even read
slowly. By moving his head kinesthetically, he could form the discrete spots into unified pictures. If his head was held still, he could
not form a total impression, merely: spots — higher, lower, right or
left of each other, thin or thick, large or small, short or long, nearer
or farther from each other. Cassirer concluded:

> Whereas normally all particular perceptions stand in a kind of ideal
> unity of meaning, through which they are held together, very much as the
> meaning of a sentence embraces the particular interpretations of its sep-
> arate words and contains them as factors in itself — in these cases of
> agnosia they seem to break apart. More and more the continuum of sig-
> nification dissolves into a series of mere points. It is not the particular sen-
> sory phenomenon as such, but the syntactical organization of these phe-
> nomena that seems to be dislocated.[11]

What is unique about this case is that the veteran trained himself
through discursive logical techniques to reconstruct his intuitional
world so that he could function, even though his basic neurological
equipment had been destroyed. In much the same way, we can understand how sufferers from dyslexia, a disturbance resulting in the
inability to read, can be helped by special training. Through this
help, the individual is taught to use more nonvisual cues to extract
meaning from letters and words, which do not go together automatically to form recognizable orthographic patterns. At the intuitive symbolic level, the unity of the perceptual experience is interdicted. If, however, the individual has already developed powers of
reasoning, cognition can be developed through other means to
overcome the limitations of the neurological insult.

In addition to the examples given above, Cassirer cited others involving apraxia, which are disabilities of action. The many examples given to illustrate his contentions are cited from the work of
Head, Gelb and Goldstein, Karl Heilbronner, and Pierre Marie. In
apraxia, especially in ideational apraxia, patients can perform
many routine actions when practical circumstances necessitate, for
example, turning a key in a lock, flicking a light switch, pouring a
glass of water. But when asked to do so, or often even when they
are asked casually to identify an object's function, they can not.

The task requires will, a sense of future possibilities, a plan of action, in short, an act of conscious thought; these patients lack the productive imagination, the ability to interchange the present and the nonpresent, the existing and the possible.[12]

These impairments cannot be conceived as a loss of particular functional skills — sensory, motor, or linguistic. As Head reiterated, to argue against faculty psychology, here was no loss of specific faculties but rather the transformation of a basic and intellectual process. Even reading and writing were often not lost as skills *per se,* according to Head:

A text may be successfully copied if every letter can simply be reproduced, stroke for stroke; but a shift from one kind of writing to another, the change for example from printing to handwriting is difficult or impossible. Spontaneous writing may be gravely impeded, although the patient may still write relatively well from dictation.[13]

What seems to be exemplified in so many of these examples is a loss that centers on the inability to see context, to differentiate the essential from the nonessential, to overcome immediacy of perception, to look beyond oneself to the totality of experience, and finally to judge action and need in the light of diverse factors having a hierarchy of relevant details. What we are seeing in these pathological cases is not necessarily a lowering of human intelligence in a global sense, but disfunctions that reveal to us the particular nature of intelligence. Each diverse example highlights, through its various revelations of cognitive loss, what intelligence could give rise to. Like tests of cognitive ability, they point to a "g" (general intellectual ability) and in so doing reveal a peculiarly human form of symbolic capacity.

Cassirer resolutely turned away any imputation that there is a basic symbolic faculty underlying man's most general cognitive skills. Rather, we must search for its meaning in terms of the function for man to which it points. What are the meanings of the "pathology of the symbolic consciousness" for a philosophy of culture? According to Cassirer:

All knowledge of the world, and all strictly spiritual action upon the world require that the I thrust the word back from itself, that in contemplation as in action it gain a certain distance from it. Animals do not know this distance: the animal *lives* in his environment; he does not place himself over against it and so represent it. The acquisition of the world as idea is, rather, the aim and product of the symbolic forms — the result of language, myth, religion, art, and theoretical knowledge. Each of these builds up its own intelligible realm of intrinsic meaning, which stands out sharply and clearly from any merely purposive behavior within the biological sphere.[14]

What Cassirer seemed to be comparing between normal human and animal behavior did not necessarily constitute a parallel between the regression symptomized in pathological behavior of the aphasiac type and lower forms of animal behavior. He recognized that the differences between man and animal were far more fundamental in structure and function than could be seen in this reduction in human autonomy. The whole realm of instinct and the closeness in adaptation to the environment that is characteristic of animal life are missing for the aphasiac.

The significant aspect of these wounded humans is the fact that the "concrete" attitude, as Goldstein was henceforth likely to describe this state, constituted a locus of behavior that contrasted so clearly to the overall significance of the behavior of normal man. Here, we see in man's fullest realization of his identity as a person, a characteristic that fills out the most prosaic and secular domain of commonsense social life — his perceptual and linguistic symbolic capacity. This potentiality will be capable of development, amplification, and differentiation into the major creative modalities of cultural life. Man achieves this symbolic integration so easily, so spontaneously. It is his unique "differentiation," the capacity for productive thought, in the best Kantian sense. And what begins in such a humble, yet richly complex, manner will go on to create worlds of experience that cannot be predicted from one generation to the next.

What this excursion into the medical realm seemed to do for Cassirer was to reveal, as no abstract work on the psychology or phenomenology of experience and thought could, some of the deeper implications of his work in the theory of knowledge and the symbolic forms. He wrote: "The process of spiritualization, the process of the world's 'symbolization,' discloses its value and meaning where it no longer operates free and unhindered, but must struggle and make its way against obstacles. In this sense, the pathology of speech and action gives us a standard by which to measure the distance separating the organic world and the world of human culture, the sphere of life and the sphere of the objective spirit."[15]

III   A Conception of Human Nature

The foregoing words represent the final development in Cassirer's conception of the relation of symbolic thought to culture, before he was thrust out of his position at Hamburg and sent into exile by Hitler (1933). Fifteen years intervened (1929–1944) before the publication of *An Essay on Man,* which constituted a summary as well as an extension of his theory of symbolic forms. In the years from 1930 to 1943 he wrote fifty major articles and reviews (including several long monographs) plus seven books. The latter were *The Philosophy of the Enlightenment* (1932), *The Platonic Renaissance in England* (1932), *Determinism and Indeterminism in Modern Physics* (1936), *Descartes* (1939), *Axel Hagerström* (1939), *The Problem of Knowledge,* Volume 4 (1940), and *The Logic of the Humanities* (1942). During this period, he lived in England, taught for several years in Sweden, then came to the United States in 1941.

Except for the final book, *The Logic of the Humanities,* he had little opportunity to explore further some of the issues that had been raised in *The Philosophy of Symbolic Forms.* And even in this book, the tenor is more humanistic and historical than it is systematic. As Cassirer was wont to reiterate, the philosopher of culture must not only classify the strands that constitute culture's diversity; he must investigate the problem of the unity of culture.

Both aspects had certain residual questions: (1) how does the intuitive status of symbolic thought as seen through aphasic and apractic pathologies as well as animal behavior give us a sense of the unique structure of human behavior? (2) how can we understand the regressive tendencies reflected in expressive and mythic behavior as it relates to both the higher development of cultural forms and that basic representational level described in the third volume of *The Philosophy of Symbolic Forms?* It is interesting to note that the first question receives fairly extensive treatment in *An Essay on Man* and is referred to in *The Logic of the Humanities.*

The problem posed in (2) is briefly recognized in *An Essay On Man.* Cassirer declares, "In human experience we by no means find the various activities which constitute the world of culture existing in harmony. On the contrary, we find the perpetual strife of diverse conflicting forces. Scientific thought contradicts and suppresses mythical thought. Religion in its highest theoretical and ethical development is under the necessity of defending the purity of its own ideal against the extravagant fancies of myth or art.''[16]

However, in *The Myth of the State*, the issue and the problems of (2) are recognized directly. Cassirer can do no more than to urge unrelenting vigilance against the subterranean powers that undercut the work of reason and civilization. In a sense, we are left here with a loose strand. How does expressive thought, as exemplified in the fears, passions, and subsuming identities of myth, relate to the sober integrative behavior of representational thought? Both seem to reside equally in that early developmental and historical time in man's career. To understand this issue, we need to explore both the psychological as well as historical depths. What Cassirer did for representational thought through his research into aphasia is needed here, too. And again, he is sensitive to this requirement as well:

In describing the structure of language, myth, religion, art, and science, we feel the constant need of a psychological terminology. We speak of religious "feeling" of artistic or mythical "imagination," of logical or rational thought.... Even more valuable seems to be the help we get from the study of general sociology. We cannot understand the form of primitive mythical thought without taking into consideration the forms of primitive society. And more urgent still is the use of historical methods. The question as to what language, myth, and religion "are" cannot be answered without a penetrating study of their historical development.[17]

If one of these two issues has priority it must be in tune with the philosophical method. The first is the more general theoretical issue. This factor is reflected in *An Essay on Man*, where the larger question of human context is subjected to Cassirer's method. And while the problem of man as *animal symbolicum* is posed and the problematics broached by definition are raised, the issues, though squarely put, are not resolved. The reason for this is perhaps twofold.

First, Cassirer's hegira upon his expulsion from his beloved German cultural homeland and his difficulty of adjusting to several new national cultures were certainly factors. Added to these were his interests in history and the philosophy of physics. These various concerns could not merely be shelved. Cassirer was fifty-five when the final volume of *The Philosophy of Symbolic Forms* was completed, and fifty-nine when he was expelled from Germany, having in the interval completed two additional books; he was almost seventy years old when he finally arrived in that most foreign of nations, the United States.

Second, these issues involving biological, psychological, and historical methods of a wholly new category of research truly demanded the energies of a much younger man. Latent in these problems was a totally new symbolic form, even now to be created, in the study of the biological roots of man's cultural achievements. Even if we must reject, as Cassirer did, the reductionist tendencies in Freud, certainly, as Susanne Langer has noted, much in Cassirer's own theory of myth echoes Freud's description of the unconscious.[18]

In addition, away from the contexts of German psychological idealism and rationalism, his orientation toward the symbolic character of human functioning was an odd perspective for one to take. The United States was bemused by behaviorism and so-called scientific psychology not far removed from some of the sensationalistic and empiricistic concerns against which Cassirer fought for many years. And though he quoted from *Human Nature and Conduct* by the ambivalent John Dewey on the issue of instinct, the position Cassirer outlined in English in *An Essay on Man* for his American audience received a respectful if not enthusiastic assent in the United States.[19]

No doubt exposure to the problem of aphasia brought Cassirer to a new perspective of symbolic thought and knowledge. And though much is devoted in Volume 3 of *The Philosophy of Symbolic Forms* to the traditional rationalist-empiricist concern about the status of commonsense knowledge, the awareness of the "pathology of the symbolic consciousness" and of its significance for understanding intuitive representation seems to have brought that debate to a culmination and conclusion, at least in Cassirer's work.

Henceforth, especially in *An Essay on Man,* there is reflected this awareness and concern for the context and sources of symbolic thought. He constantly reiterated, and with justification, that he was not interested in substantial explanations (such as the hypotheses of Kurt Goldstein), that symbolic thought is rooted in man's recent phylogenetic acquisition of the frontal lobes of the brain.[20] And he rightly pushed away from brain pathology, truly an important example, but ultimately a side road in the quest for understanding about human nature and culture.

It is typical, if still amazing, that Cassirer, in making the transfer from Europe to America, and in having to bridge such different perspectives on such a broad issue as human nature, came to what is even today a completely reliable presentation of the issues. Ultimately, an understanding of culture and man's symbolic propensities, which give rise to culture, must be rooted in a theoretical context. The deontologizing process in the study of knowledge and culture has brought us step by step to this point. By lifting the veils that hide the logical character of each symbolic modality, we have learned what, for example, makes myth a discrete symbolic form and what seems to unite it with the other forms of culture, both comparatively and historically.

But now we must go further. We understand how the basic character of perceptual experience is mediated symbolically. Man is a symbolic animal. But he is also part of life itself. And, as Cassirer had noted in *The Problem of Knowledge,* biology had become a science in its own right, with problems, subject matter, and theories from which was carved out a domain of thought that could not be reduced to either metaphysical or physico-chemical forms: "The struggle between mechanism and vitalism has brought science no nearer to an explanation of the 'essence of life.' But it has compelled biology again and again to examine the question concerning 'its own nature as a science' and thus to gain a clearer knowledge of its own specific task and of the methods of thought which are especially suited to its accomplishment."[21]

Biology thus has both structural and historical aspects. One of the questions that inevitably arises is that of function. And it is likely that the question that Cassirer placed for man — the meaning and locus of his pattern of communication and expression — will be asked of other forms of life. Is not symbolism a principle that one may trace back to a much deeper source and that has a much broader range of applicability.[22] And as he reflected further, if we answer this question in the negative and avoid the issue of historic or evolutionary origins as well as the structural concomitants, then have we not left the structure of human culture in a uniquely isolated position?

Drawing from the work of the American Charles Morris, and his theory of communication, Cassirer made this crucial distinction between animal and human behavior, a distinction that marks that clear boundary line of theory that must be crossed before the problem of human nature can be resolved: "Symbols in the proper sense of this term — cannot be reduced to signals. Signals and symbols belong to two different universes of discourse: a signal is a part of the physical world of being; a symbol is a part of the human world of meaning. Signals are 'operators'; symbols are 'designators.'"[23]

Here, the physical world of being relates signals to functions, which are to serve the basic adaptive needs of the animal. These adaptive needs are dictated by the genetic structure of the creature. Such behaviors are out of the realm of conscious control. The signals by which animals communicate elicit responses that are so exclusively meant for survival that no animal can exercise independent action. The signals are automatic elicitors drawn from the environmental context and surrendered to by the animal through genetically rooted responses.

Drawing upon the work of Edward Thorndike, W. Koehler, and R.M. Yerkes, as well as the German biologist Johannes von Uexküll, Cassirer saw this problem as an insuperable theoretical antinomy, a paradox for man. His classical expression of it is as follows:

Man has, as it were, discovered a new method of adapting himself to his environment. Between the receptor system and the effector system, which are to be found in all animal species, we find in man a third link which we may describe as the "symbolic system." This new acquisition transforms the whole of human life. As compared with other animals man lives not merely in a broader reality; he lives, so to speak, in a new 'dimension' of reality. There is an unmistakable difference between organic reactions and human responses. In the first case, a direct and immediate answer is given to an outward stimulus; in the second case the answer is delayed. It is interrupted and retarded by a slow and complicated process of thought. At first sight such a delay may appear to be a very questionable gain. Many philosophers have warned against this pretended progress. "L'homme qui médite," says Rousseau, "èst un animal dépravé": it is not an improvement but a deterioration of human nature to exceed the boundaries of organic life.[24]

It is obvious from the many American authorities and citations that Cassirer, in the short time that he lived in the United States, had read widely. And most probably, he was aware that the scientists and theoreticians dealing with these issues of culture and man had come to a set of widely differing conclusions based on a far different intellectual context than the one that had been influential in creating Cassirer's Marburg neo-Kantianism. In fact, the combination of psychological empiricism and Darwinian evolutionism produced this very different structure of ideas — behaviorism.

One can almost see the two traditions coming up against each other in dialectical opposition; the one, continental and humanistic, taking its perspectives from Kant and Hegel and the rich humanistic tradition surrounding them, a product of centuries of creative, imaginative continental thought since the Renaissance; the other, Anglo-American in orientation, practical, pragmatic, being influenced by the enormous technological and economic forces of change let loose in the nineteenth and twentieth century, yet deeply concerned to see practice and theory wedded to each other. This tradition was more in debt to Benjamin Franklin, John Stuart Mill, and Charles Darwin than to the continentals.

It was perhaps this new dialectical issue that forced Cassirer to reject both ends of this theoretical continuum. The idealist, whether represented by vitalists such as Hans Driesch, whose concept of "entelechy" argued for an inner purposefulness in biological processes incorporating physicochemical processes in fulfilling these inner tendencies, or Johannes Uexküll, whose concept of inner form or structure, seemed to go beyond the scope of the empirical evidence to explain their theories.[25] To Cassirer, it was a theoretical efflorescence to explain the behavior of organisms in terms of what could be seen only as a series of gratuitous *ad hoc* metaphysical concepts from the standpoint of practical efficiency. Certainly, the imposition of a principle of economy, an Occam's razor, would reveal the disfunctionality of such principles. And yet, Cassirer was sensitive to the idealists' concern, that the world of human values should not be overwhelmed by the raw mechanism, or tooth and claw realities, of the lower biological world. Rather than mental life being reduced to survivalistic function, a way must be found to carve out a domain of autonomy for life from its physicochemical matrix, a way to establish a principle of evolutionary directiveness that would maintain human culture in its position as the final culmination of living purpose and not as an irrelevant pathway in a maze of evolutionary trails, randomly utilized or abandoned by nature.

It was obvious to Cassirer when he was writing *The Problem of Knowledge* and even later in *An Essay on Man* that the "vitalistic" tradition was waning. The steady drift of evidence, in spite of a variety of heroic efforts, seemed to dissipate all claims for inner dynamic and autonomous processes in organic behavior. Yet he was obviously sympathetic to the anti-reductivist fears of this group; he responded especially to Uexküll's concern for the autonomy of form and behavior in life but did not draw the same metaphysical conclusions from Uexküll's almost phenomenalistic analysis of organic behavior and function.

The great challenge came from the other side, from the new behaviorism and reductionism that was so dominant in his newly adopted land. What struck him here was the concern for the continuity of nature. It had to be that these scientists, themselves men of fine education and culture, were cognizant of their own intellectual uniqueness. Yet they tried to surmount a built-in bias by attempting to account for the experimental facts of organic structure and behavior in terms of the demands of this most persuasive theoretical structure. Specifically, the interpretation of Darwinism dominant during the 1940s argued that all life was subjected inexorably to the principles of mutation, adaptation, and natural selection. The interpretation of adaptation as it applied to all living things saw adaptation fulfilled in bringing to reproductive maturity the young of all species. These practical requirements applied in terms of individual as well as species-wide behavior.

It seemed that little could be done to bend the theory of evolution so that it could more easily incorporate some of the most basic assumptions of the European humanistic tradition. What was man, after all? At most, he was a million-year afterthought of a process that had been proceeding with lawlike regularity and inexorability for several billion years. The behavioristic search, then, was not for a theory of man that would save the distinctiveness of culture for the humanistic tradition but one that would take man off his imperial perch and place him down in the arena of organic evolution with the rest of the animals.

The effect was to neutralize the implicit uniqueness of man and reduce culture to a manifestation of some organic dissatisfaction. It was also, and more seriously for Cassirer's views, to see culture as a product. In effect, it removed the autonomy of thought and the status of culture as a creation of man, *sui generis.* If man's evolutionary role was to adapt to the environment to further his biological perdurance, then culture was a response to environmental challenges, a unique biologically rooted attribute of man whose character and evolution had to be seen and evaluated in terms of its adaptation to these external demands.

As we have seen from the previous citations from Cassirer's *An Essay on Man,* this view of man as mere responder to be manipulated by the force of the environment was not acceptable. Culture and the symbolic forms would here have to be analyzed in terms of their serving the adaptation of the organism, as rising to the challenge of natural selection. Instead of evaluating art, religion, and science in terms of intrinsic human needs, one would expect a more direct environmental challenge to be met. This is not to argue against Cassirer's view that the symbolic forms as products of man are in some manner related to man's basic structural character, a character that is ultimately the product of evolutionary forces.

Thus, at the heart of Cassirer's turning away from the dominant American view of human behavior was its crass and simplistic attempt to circumvent the richness and complexity of man's behavior, to see it merely in terms of a "white rat" in a cage. This attitude is exemplified in his subtle use of citations from John Dewey, who himself turned away from the extreme behavioristic wing of scientific psychology.[26] It is true also of Edward Thorndike who, in spite of his "connectivism," recognized some of those theoretically significant differences in psychological motivation that, for example, could be understood in terms of signal and symbolic behavior.[27]

Yet it would not be fair to say that the perspectives in the United States during that time were all one way. The numerous refugee psychologists, many of them advocates of Gestalt psychology, did lend a softening quality to the intellectual milieu. Men such as Kurt Lewin, Koffka, Köhler, Heinz Werner (a Cassirer student), were well respected. In addition, the psychoanalytic scene contributed a number of researchers who disagreed with Freud's early concentration on drives. Ego psychologists such as Karen Horney and Erich Fromm were popular disseminators of a hopeful rationalism. The impact of cultural anthropology displayed to the American intellectual scene a picture of a variety of simple cultures, close to nature and nature's survivalistic demands, cultures, however, almost indifferent to the challenges to adapt and rise up, in their preoccupation with rite, religion, art, and play or war.

It is interesting to note that those contributors to the *Ernst Cassirer* volume, edited by P. A. Schilpp in 1949, who were concerned with the issue of culture versus nature felt the need to argue that Cassirer had trodden onto shifting sands when he held out against the absorption of culture into nature. I. K. Stephens, for example, criticized Cassirer for making man's "will to logic" central, and overlooking the "will to live." In fact, he felt that Cassirer had neglected the whole operation of evolutionary adaptation.[28]

David Bidney, in a long essay on Cassirer's plilosophical anthropology, also noted the seeming apposition of culture and nature as well as Cassirer's approach to what in the anthropological debates of that era was termed the superorganicist position. This term, coined years earlier by A. E. Kroeber, was espoused in the 1940s by Leslie White and his followers of the Michigan school of anthropology.[29] The superorganicists held that the laws of culture are autonomous, that one need not root them in the texture of evolutionary theory. In terms of research methodology, Leslie White argued the theories of anthropology were as much dependent on, or independent of, the concept structure of physics and chemistry as was biology itself.

Cassirer did not, in holding to the distinctiveness of man's symbolic nature, mean to oppose man and nature or to propose a break in the laws of evolution that heralded *Homo sapiens* coming to be. Man was part of nature and that included the organic world. What he opposed was the simplistic conception of behavior into which some theoreticians wanted to dissolve man and culture. At no point did he feel that the theoretical conceptions through which the theory of evolution was at that time being expressed were complete enough to prevent the expansiveness of nature from being violated by the apposition of behavioral and cultural models.

Perhaps the model of explanation that was presently being used to describe animal behavior was satisfactory for the experimental work then in progress. Today, we realize in our ethnological observations that animals in the wild behave differently from those in zoos or in laboratories. This realization, in turn, has led to variations in our conceptual understanding of animal behavior as compared with thirty years ago. The key issue about which Cassirer was concerned was the general theory of evolution, which encompassed the broadest injunction to scientists to search for regularities within the guidelines of the Darwinian trinity: mutation, adaptation, and natural selection. These concepts were being applied as holy writ with an almost scholastic rigidity.

The theory of evolution constituted no reality. It is a conceptual structure that in organizing Darwin's wide-ranging naturalistic experience sets forth certain anticipations about future research. It is merely a theoretical statement of what should and will be found in the process of empirical research. If evidence is found that runs counter to these expectations, then the current structure must adjust. If the basic assumptions collapse under the weight of such new emendations, this result will merely facilitate the development of newer and more universal principles.

Cassirer observed that the present application of Darwin that would envelop symbolic behavior and culture in a simple ritual of survival violates too great a corpus of evidence. The theory, he believed, is in need of amplification or revision to meet the huge accumulation of knowledge that we have obtained. Man is part of organic reality, and the transition from signal behavior and stimulus response (receptor-effector) relationships to symbol and culture must be given historical and cultural flesh. But:

> The logical analysis of human speech always leads us to an element of prime importance which has no parallel in the animal world. The general theory of evolution in no sense stands in the way of the acknowledgment of this fact. Even in the field of the phenomena of organic nature we have learned that evolution does not exclude a sort of original creation. The fact of sudden mutation and of emergent evolution has to be admitted. Modern biology no longer speaks of evolution in terms of earlier Darwinism; nor does it explain the causes of evolution in the same way. We may readily admit that the anthropoid apes, in the development of certain symbolic processes, have made a significant forward step. But again we must insist that they did not reach the threshold of the human world. They entered as it were, a blind alley.[30]

Cassirer was here expressing the faith that though the theoretical construction that could bring the conception of symbolic function into the evolutionary context admittedly was not yet available, it will one day be so. One can liken this state of theory-building to that classic example of scientific methodology at work—the discovery of the planet Neptune. It was discovered that the motion of the planet Uranus was puite irregular. Charts that were being developed in 1820 by the French scientist Bouvard after the Laplaceian model were hampered by the puzzling evidence of Uranus, whose motions were so unlike the regularities of its neighbors Saturn and Jupiter. At first, it was thought that earlier observations and/or the compilation of tables might have been in error. Over a period of several years of new and intense observation and calculation, many of these irregularities were confirmed by other scientists. Another set of possibilites was put forth as explanation, including the hypothetical possibility of error in the computation of the mass of Saturn.

As one by one these hypotheses were discarded, a most conjectural idea began to intrude with increasing force — the possibility of the existence of an ultra-Uranian planet, whose phantom presence exerted a gravitational influence over the motions of Uranus. More years of conjecture occurred, then came several hesitant mathematical attempts to calculate the location of this hypothetical planet. Finally, in 1846, again after several observational attempts, the planet was located. Researchers from four nations, including the American Benjamin Peirce, the father of the philosopher C. S. Peirce, contributed to this discovery. It is significant that the possibility of the existence of Neptune had been suggested for over twenty years but could not be intensely pursued until the more obvious theories had had their chance.

This example is particularly important for philosophy because philosophy is the most general and encompassing of all forms of thought. Its purpose is to reveal the most general shape of things, to make connections and to anticipate issues and facts. Philosophy should have heuristic value in what it uncovers for thought, and in how it disciplines us to refrain from jumping on one contemporary intellectual bandwagon after another, in short, to wait until all the facts have come in.

This is preface to arguing that the past thirty years have demonstrated the rightness of Cassirer's intuition on these matters, and ultimately the soundness of his views on knowledge, the structure of theory, and the concept of symbolic form. As has been shown in some detail elsewhere, his implicit expectations have been confirmed experimentally and theoretically and have now entered the corpus of evolutionary literature as a central tenet of our understanding of human behavior.[31] In fact, it is not unfair to say that there has been a sharp decline in the explanatory persuasiveness of behaviorist and reductionist theories and a resurgence of interest in rationalistic views as well as in theories concerned with the inner structure represented in the dynamics of human behavior.[32]

The issue on which the evolutionary interpretation of culture has turned has been over the extent to which the morphological uniqueness of man's brain, and presumably his capacity for language and culture, was a product of close selective molding. If that were the case, as it must be, for the myriad of practical organic structures in all creatures, then we should see in language and culture a clear concrete and adaptive function. At this point the ingenious work of behavioristic psychologists and social scientists began. Darwin says: survival of the species depends of adaptation to the environment and consequent natural selection through random external forces leading to the successful reproduction of the species. Thus the cultural products of the brain must have tangible selective power for the species.

This belief has led one important authority in evolutionary genetics to argue that musical talent, seeing that it is valued in culture, must have a special selective value for *Homo sapiens* and have negative selective impact on those individuals who are relatively bereft of these specific skills.[33] One need not deny that culture has been a successful vehicle for human expression. But to argue that specific human skills have specific selective value is, first, to draw the theory too tightly around a few factual issues, and, second, to blind oneself to some of the empirical realities as they exist in our society.

New interpretations of the process of evolution and a careful consideration of the facts have brought forth issues that vitiate the attempt to see in human culture a replication of the tooth and claw view of behavior. According to more recent approaches, an adaptive and selective advantage for brain size and complexity is seen in the forerunners of man. The matter of evasive behavior and care of the young all go along with environmental awareness, good vision, and audition as well as concern for the survival of the family group. These elements, carefully selected out for many millions of years, were probably released from close environmental pressures about two to five million years ago so that so-called orthoselective trends, the continuation in mutation of one pattern of evolution, proceeded on its own.[34] The precipitous growth of the brain was a result.[35] And with this came the revolutionary alteration of human behavior, communication, social interaction, from the signal system to the symbol system.

At this point, entirely new sets of adaptive responses must have begun to take place. These interactions of social and natural factors are no doubt going on at this very time. The thrust of the new view of human evolution is not that at every step of human evolution a cultural invention — a tool — had immediate feedback for the genetic advantage or disadvantage of individuals or groups. The hypothesis is that if culture, high or low, has a selective advantage, it is in the main a man-made advantage. For certainly, as A. R. Wallace noted long ago, in nature it makes little difference for phylogenetic survival that man have a 1400 cubic centimeter brain rather than one of 700 or 900 cubic centimeters.[36] The brain must have developed rapidly and independently of direct environmental pressures.

The result is a set of human behaviors that must be rooted in the morphology of man, in those inner structures and processes that constitute man's unique evolutionary heritage and nature. The process is a naturalistic one, not to be explained through metaphysical constructs. The difficulty now lies in explaining human behavior in terms of man's cultural uniqueness as well as his biological inheritance. Cassirer was probably correct in warning us away from any simple structural or substantialistic explanations of symbolic behavior as that inhering, for example, in the frontal lobes or cerebral cortex of the brain or in any other specific substantial source. This search for material origins, dangerous as such in its theoretical simplicity, constitutes a commitment to a specific explanatory anchor at too early a stage in the evolution of this science.

Cassirer's search for the inner logical law that undergirded the development of each symbolic form forced him to face up to the problems of the connectivity of cultural patterns and of their larger philosophical context, that is, to what all this meant in theory. The realization of how far back symbolic activity could be traced in man and the fact that art, religion, science, history, and logic all began with the basic human propensity to experience the world symbolically, resulted in the concept of *animal symbolicum*. This concept now placed the issue of culture into the context of evolution. Cassirer's refusal to allow the symbol to be effaced in a superficial behavioral reading of the evolutionary doctrine led to a whole new set of empirical and theoretical issues.[37]

Culture and man's symbolic abilities out of which culture develops have created our scientific structure of inquiry. Through neurological, genetic, and psycholinguistic studies we now enquire into the structural basis for those symbolic activities which we view as macroscopic historical achievements — that is, as art, religion, and technology. Just as the study of aphasic patients revealed the enormous delicacy of man's intellectual achievements through the example of the disintegration of behavior, the challenge now is to understand culture and man's unique social achievements in terms of their inner psychobiological character. (Macroanalysis leads to microanalysis of macroachievement.)

This new world of research and the empirical and theoretical problems it will generate exemplify the enlarging network of symbolic forms that can evolve in man's creative dialectic with social and natural experience. Here is demonstrated that familiar Cassirerean paradox, that in each empirical or theoretical advance we see man simultaneously turning into himself in his creative quest. Again, the growth of culture outward, at the same time, reflects a deepening involvement with the problem of the inner laws of advance.

IV   *Conflict in Man and Culture*

The symbolic view of human nature that Cassirer set forth to contrast with reductive biological interpretations easily fits into his larger view of knowledge as a creative and open-ended dimension of human culture. We have here a view of human nature that from its origins in the evolutionary process to its contemporary complexity and richness is logically consistent. Man the animal is free of anterior drives and purely practical survivalistic motives. Man the cultural being envisages the forms of knowing and creating without conforming to an external criterion of being or a material substrate of sensations.

Everywhere materiality — tools, perceptions, sounds, tastes, objects to be touched and fondled — becomes a means or a pivot in the process of symbolic envisagement. It is invested with meaning, structure, and significance. There are no limits to its symbolic possibilities. We can only in vague and general terms perceive the laws and principles guiding the outward expansion and multiplication of symbolic forms and the ever-deepening richness of meaning, the ideal articulations of which the human spirit is capable.

But is this picture of man that Cassirer delineated accurate or complete? It is, as Fritz Kaufmann has noted, an Apollonian vision of the possibilities inherent in man.[38] It hardly touches on another aspect, the darker, paradoxical, and ultimately finite limitations inherent in this creature. Turning from this dimming picture of the individual person to the problem of culture, we are aware of another missing dimension. In the phenomenological development of the symbolic forms of thought, do we truly have an accurate picture of the dynamics of culture? We see the progress, the steady distillation of the inner logical purity of each form as it develops historically in the various cultural modalities. But underneath this sense of progress, is there only calm, no struggle, conflict, or even defeat?

This, in essence, is the great problem in Cassirer's neo-Kantian vision of man and culture. It is echoed many times over by both admirers and critics. The message is fairly consistent in spite of the various approaches to different aspects of his theory and the varying points of view of the critics. John Herman Randall, an historian of philosophy with a pragmatic and naturalist point of view, can complain that Cassirer, in analyzing the progress and the spirit of an age, seems totally unconcerned with "any question of historical causation" or with the dynamics of historical change such that one could discern the impact of technological or economic matters in historical change. "Economic determinism is not so much as mentioned. Indeed, it is hard to ascertain whether the social sciences and their subject matter enter into Cassirer's thought at all," complains Randall.[39] In a similar vein, the educational philosopher Theodore Brameld, after analyzing Cassirer's philosophy of culture, subjects it to a Deweyan pragmatic test of its impact on the ongoing development of a democratic society. The neo-Kantian view of the autonomy of spirit, he argues, neglects the manner in which language and religion become foci for economic and political power dynamics. We need to know how these factors interact between individual and society, and we need to know how we can choose, or value, so as to affirm clear-cut democratic values.[40] Because Cassirer paid little attention to the struggle for freedom as it engages in the social and institutional forms of life as well as the aesthetic and intellectual, Brameld argues that Cassirer's faith in man's rationality is limited to "the polite virtues of a cultivated and rational civilization."[41]

These criticisms hint at the lack of normative focus in Cassirer's philosophy and his unwillingness to argue for a specific direction for society or for man. Cassirer seemed to be confident that the direction ultimately embodied in civilization will reflect man's inner nature and his creative search for symbolic envisagement. The difference in the pragmatic view is (1) a lack of confidence that the ultimate realization of social change will be a productive culture, unless there is at the same time a struggle to create a just social order; and (2) a hesitation that the essence of man and culture can be realized in the symbolic and rational view that Cassirer envisioned unless there is at the same time a struggle to create a just social order; and (2) a hesitation that the essence of man and culture can be realized in the symbolic and rational view that Cassirer envisioned unless certain practical methodologies for thought and action are tangibly and normatively enacted in the world. Cassirer seemed to expect, with the exception of his presentation in *The Myth of the State,* that natural cultural processes will determine in their dialectical rhythms the ultimate state of man and culture.

with regard to humanity and culture, focuses on the problem of the individual. In Cassirer's writings, many important and great individuals are represented. Yet they all seem to ride a crest of cultural advance. One can almost view them as purveyors of deep intellectual traditions, problems, and movements, rather than as individuals battling against tradition to bring forth their view of the truth. Because truth is relative to the age, the process of cultural evolution appears to be acting through the individual rather than the latter being the efficient and independent agent fighting for change. According to Helmut Kuhn.

For Cassirer, life comes into view only as *"vita acta,"* 'life that was lived," never as *"vita agenda,"* "life as it is to be lived." This accounts for the calm perfection of his thought, and also for its ineluctable limitations. He is not in the mélée, forever breathing the cool air of contemplative detachment. But how such serenity is achieved his philosophy does not tell. [42]

Kuhn discusses the chapter entitled "Tragedy of Culture" in *The Logic of the Humanities* wherein Cassirer probed some of the problematics of cultural dislocation — rise and fall — in the light of his vision of culture and the symbolic forms. To Kuhn, there is not enough of the reality of tension and tragedy even here. Individuals and events are disembodied and etherealized. It is an abstract vision, one unmarred by human misery or real tragedy. Kuhn argues as follows:

With one glance we embrace the Symbolic Forms, a solemn array of structures which outline the timeless possibilities of the creative mind. Their rigid architecture rises above an element of infinite mobility, a whirl of incessant change: the temporal flux of life. At brief creative moments this flux is arrested. It crystallizes into shapes that temporarily fill the vessels of timeless possibility with the actuality of life: languages become articulate, religions seek and find credence, works of art spread delight, philosophies express truth. But life is alternation of building up and breaking down. Man's creations, the works of culture, bask for a while in the broad daylight of history only to return whence they came. Such is "the tragedy of culture," according to Cassirer.... For the twentieth century scholar, the timeless validity of symbolic structures is not enough to forestall tragedy, because the old imperious desire for "world without end" is not entirely put to sleep. The individual is not wholly banished. His ghost-like presence suffuses the great unconcern of the philosophy of Symbolic Forms with an elegiac mood.[43]

Not enough is evident, so this genre of criticism goes, of the real passions and needs of concrete individuals or of their power in the light of their limitations and personal drives. When Cassirer attempted to trace the phenomenology of the creative spirit in terms of its internal patterns of symbolic envisagement, he was overlooking that voluntaristic dimension in which the demands are perhaps symbolic too, but overlaid with different social and psychological intentions. Here perhaps are those forces that give rise to other, more destructive, finite elements in man and culture than he was at first ready to admit.

In an extended and masterful analysis of Cassirer that appears in the Schilpp volume "Cassirer, Neo-Kantianism, and Phenomenology," Fritz Kaufmann goes furthest in placing Cassirer's view in the perspective of a philosophical tradition, phenomenology and existentialism, that overtook and ultimately by-passed neo-Kantianism as an attractive and persuasive position for young intellectuals of the mid-twentieth century. Many intellectuals were increasingly suspicious of the results of Western civilization, even in the context of its great cultural achievements. Yet greater disturbances and violations of the human spirit have since occurred. Cassirer was, however, drawn to normality and the open and undisturbed functions of thought. Even as in his work on aphasia, the pathological was a means of establishing knowledge of the normal. Fritz Kaufmann compared Cassirer with Kant, noting that they both breathe the spiritual outlook on life. What Cassirer said about Kant can be directed equally at him: He ... "is and remains a thinker of the 'Enlightenment' in the most radiant and sublime sense of this word: he aspires toward light and clarity even when reflecting on the darkest depths and 'radices' of being."[44]

It is this pain that is in life that Kaufmann finds neglected in Cassirer. The philosopher searches for the formative power of thought, for the productivity and creativity in the human soul. Here he finds human freedom and glories in its infinite possibilities. At the same time, he misses the abyss that is freedom, "that freedom which is, at once, man's destruction and his temptation, man's pride and his torment — and he does not ask how human freedom can coexist with human finiteness."[45]

As Kaufmann put it further, Cassirer saw the progression of man out of the limitations of life as a dialectical process, proceeding in tensions and releases in the intellectual advance both outward and inward. And yet, there is so little about the "labor pains" of such a dialectical turn and thus the crisis of human existence.[46] The perceptions of Cassirer seem always turned upward toward possibilities, toward the openness and the infinite capabilities of man, culture and symbol. On the contrary, the reality of man and culture is tension, pain, and disenchantment.

Referring to Heidegger's 1928 review of the second volume of *The Philosophy of Symbolic Forms,* Kaufmann notes Heidegger's view that myth provides a notable opportunity to pursue the systematic unity of human existence (*Lebensform*). Rather than viewing myth as the creative first step upward toward the fuller elucidation of the symbolic powers of man, myth reveals to us an ultimate limit. The concept of "mana" which to Cassirer begins the process of drawing logical distinctions and separating the face of experience into intentional categories, can be seen not as prolegomena but rather as an ultimate category of human perplexity. Rather than a creative organ of self expression aiding in the articulation of experience, "mana" merely reflects that fundamental sense of being overwhelmed by the world around him. And it is not enough to recognize these feelings in order to rise beyond such situations. No, the situation may be intrinsically more serious, declares Heidegger:

> The myth may thus testify to his resigning himself to the domination of uncontrollable powers as well as exhibit his constructive capacities. The world of the myth though being in one sense the work of his creative imagination, may still fail to be man's proper world — the world in which he feels at home. The needy man, the man dependent on mercy and subject to renunciation, disappears ... behind the screen of his specious cultural achievements.[47]

In short, as Kaufmann goes on to explain, while modern Continental philosophy may approve of the general concerns that Cassirer's philosophy encompasses — the problem of human nature, culture, and the process of knowing — it is his orientation to these issues that is what is found wanting. Like Kant, Cassirer is concerned with the "intelligible substrate of humanity," not with human existence. The purely personal problems and involvements of individuals as they confront the timeless crises of life and death are not touched on. We do not feel the pain that underlies existence for the average human or concern for the choices he must make day to day. The truly profound and most deeply felt experiences — love, hatred, fear, trembling, shame, repentance, guilt, and sin, even concentration and distraction — are absorbed into the creatural forms of cultural life.[48]

Cassirer never touched on the truly meaningful and existential facets of human life that perhaps more truly reveal what man and culture are and what constitutes the major portion of existence. The external facets of culture — the products of science, art, literature, language — stand as no true revelation of the turmoil and travail that must have occurred in their creation. As with the iceberg, it is unwise to conclude that what is seen is equal to what is. One must probe below the surface to get to the substance and dimension of reality. The external facade is only one aspect, and a minor one, of the totality of cultural existence as it touches and moves human beings to action.[49]

One can argue that the mid-twentieth century, roughly coinciding with the maturity and death of Cassirer, represents a watershed era in which the divide between two philosophical approaches to man and culture met and clashed. It was an era in which the "Apollonian" view of progress, change, and optimism, underlined in a deep commitment to reason and science, was bested by those philosophies that stressed conflict, self-interest, and the limitations of self-determination and reason in the confrontation of events.

In the first grouping, one could place the neo-Kantian tradition, the pragmatic and positivistic orientation of Anglo-American philosophy, and in general, that liberal, melioristic social tradition that derived from the Enlightenment. The second tradition included both phenomenology and existentialism, plus a variety of pessimistic incarnations of Catholic and Protestant theology that was absorbed into this new philosophy of *Angst* and finitude. Along with this went the Marxian social and historical determinism, which emphasized the inevitability of conflict. Here too was the Freudian concern with the unconscious sources of human behavior and the limited hopes for cultural regeneration.

Only today can one appreciate the manner in which the intellectual class throughout the world has abandoned the attitudes and expectations of such thinkers as Cassirer, Dewey, and Russell, for more intimate perspectives on man. These offer immediate surcease from personal disquietude and perhaps more mechanical historical good tidings from the dialectics of economic inevitabilities and the coming revolutionary social upheavals. To be sure, the optimists, all born in a nineteenth-century context of widening intellectual horizons, could not have predicted the various social traumas of twentieth-century life, especially the holocaust of World War II. This fact could not be swept away in thought as merely another passing event on the road to a more hopeful future.

Cassirer saw the rising influence of phenomenology and existentialism taking hold in Germany even during his best years, at the University of Hamburg. In "Kant und das Problem der Metaphysik," (1931), he attempted to reply to the work of Heidegger, with whom he had debated these issues at Davos in 1929.[50] Earlier, in *"'Geist' und "Leben' in der Philosophie der Gegenwurt"* (*"Spirit" and "Life" in Contemporary Philosophy*) (1930), he dealt with the work of Max Scheler.[51] Even in Volume 3 of *The Philosophy of Symbolic Forms* there aer ample and sympathetic references to the various writers of this movement. He was making a real attempt to meet them in their own contexts. This effort was especially important to Cassirer since, in his last years, his fellow Marburger Paul Natorp had been moving his psychological investigations in a more phenomenological direction. Natorp was attempting to broaden his perspectives to the more mundane, everyday shaping of objective experience and to register it unhampered by ulterior categories from the sciences.

Cassirer's expulsion from Germany in 1933 effectively ended this dialogue. And it is only in his last work, *The Myth of the State,* that he directly confronted the darker issues of human thought and behavior. In this book, he was forced to reexamine the powerfully persuasive ideas of Sigmund Freud. And though one would think that Freud's work would throw much subsequent light on the depredations of Nazism — the topic that is the core of concern in this book — the ideas of the psychoanalyst are raised only to be refuted. At the same time, the mythological manipulations of the Nazis are described and explained in a sociohistorical context as an attempt to destroy reason and ethics through the perversion of the natural intentionality of language.

Yet, as Susanne Langer has noted, Cassirer should have seen the close affinity between his own view of mythic thinking as an independent modality of thought, an *Ur-stratum* which maintains its own status and integrity when compared with rational thought, and Freud's conception of the unconscious, the world of dreams, wishes, and fears that lies below the surface of everyday civilized life. Referring to Cassirer, Langer says, "Yet the relationship between the new psychiatry and his own new epistemology is deep and close; 'der Mythos als Denkform' is the theme that rounds out the modern philosophical picture of human mentality to embrace psychology and anthropology and linguistics, which had broken the narrow limits of rationalist theory, in a more adequate conceptual frame."[52]

Cassirer's antipathy to Freud lay not so much in the facts that Freud has revealed. Rather, it is in his placement of the facts in a scheme of human culture and then his use of these materials that concern him. Here, the issue of normative function intrudes, an aspect of Cassirer's ethical point of view that eludes Helmut Kuhn in his analysis of Cassirer's deficiencies in proposing a historical-cultural program of values. How does one propose where man should go when one believes in man's freedom to so decide. What one can do is merely to point out the errors in concept and in practice.

Freud stands as a good example of the mistaken use of factual materials in the description of man, these facts to be used later as a measure of human possibilities. As Langer puts it, Cassirer objected to the manner in which Freud reified his own practical concerns into the normative domain of culture. Since Freud

deals entirely with the evils of social maladjustment, his measure of good is simply adjustment; religion and learning and social reform, art and discovery and philosophical reflection, to him are just so many avenues of personal gratification — sublimation of passions, emotional self-expression. From his standpoint they cannot be viewed as objective values. Just as good poetry and bad poetry are of equal interest and importance to the psychoanalyst, so the various social systems are all equally good, all religions equally true (or rather, equally false, but salutary), and all abstract systems of thought, scientific or philosophical or mathematical, just self-dramatizations in disguise.[53]

Freud was also devastated by the impact of what he had himself uncovered and which he discussed in *Civilization and Its Discontents*. He was dismayed at the seeming inevitability of conflict, as between Eros and Thanatos. Cassirer was outraged by Freud's seeming assent to human limitations. It seemed to him that man was bound by the necessities of his inner nature to overcome these. Freud's error was not merely in his descriptive and practical use of the idea of the "unconscious" and its extrapolation of mythic elements but in the core principle that enabled him to generalize about the unconscious. According to Cassirer in Freudian theory "Myth was deeply rooted in human nature; it was based upon a fundamental and irresistible instinct the nature and character of which remained to be determined."[54]

It was not the empirical method that Freud used that disturbed Cassirer. Freud needed to interpret these data coherently to find the force that lay hidden behind the observable data. It was this turn of method that Cassirer attacked: "While he continued to speak as a physician and psychopathologist, he thought as a determined metaphysician."[55]

The reductive tendency in Freud alluded to by Cassirer, to see the libido of the sex drives with their implications of a biological substratum to human actions, which therefore limits and restricts human freedom, constitutes the crux of Cassirer's objections. Concerning the sex myths, such as the Oedipus complex, as analyzed by Freud, Cassirer writes, "It is not a very satisfactory explanation of a fact that has put its indelible mark upon the whole life of mankind to reduce it to a special and simple motive. Man's psychic and cultural life is not made of such simple and homogeneous stuff."[56]

But Freud's revelation of the latent and not so latent violence in man's psychic nature is certainly reflected more fearfully and transcendentally in the Nazi political myths than in Cassirer's own critical and even negative acknowledgement of them. Cassirer, like Freud, experienced the fury of the myths, suffered because of them, and was chastened and made wiser by them. Freud, in his final writings, acknowledged his own rationalistic intentions more clearly and did set forth a tempered optimism in his view that reason and the psychoanalytic method might find a way of opening the psyche to the light of intellectual enquiry and restraint. The battle would have to be fought continuously and even relentlessly.

Cassirer concomitantly acknowledged for the first time, after Heraclitus, that the "way upward was at the same time the way downward." Looking back at the depredations of the war, he had to realize more than he had before, that the "expressive" domain that lay within us could rise up, dominate, and even extinguish the higher creativity that marked the symbolic forms. Myth is invulnerable to philosophy. Cassirer had clearly spelled out its independence. But philosophy can help us to understand the enemy, to know his defects, weaknesses, and strengths, and not to underrate them:

When we first heard of the political myths we found them so absurd and incongruous, so fantastic and ludicrous that we could hardly be prevailed upon to take them seriously. By now it has become clear to all of us that this was a great mistake. We should not commit the same error a second time. We should carefully study the origin, the structure, the methods, and the techniques, of the political myths. We should see the adversary face to face in order to know how to combat him.[57]

A chastened Ernst Cassirer, in this final work, now pointed to the mysterious nature of this deeply rooted destructive force. The great masterworks of human culture "are not eternal nor unassailable. Our science, our poetry, our art, and our religion are only the upper layer of a much older stratum that reaches down to a greater depth. We must always be prepared for violent concussions that may shake our cultural world and our social order to its very foundations."[58]

As noted earlier, he spoke of the Babylonian legend wherein human culture is a product of a conquest by man over the darkness of myth.[59] But these mythic monsters were never completely destroyed. They were incorporated into another universe, (the unconscious?). As long as "forces, intellectual, ethical, and artistic are in full strength myth is tamed and subdued. But once they begin to lose their strength chaos is come again. Mythical thought then starts to rise anew and to pervade the whole of man's cultural and social life"; these were Cassirer's final words.[60]

CHAPTER 6

Cassirer in Retrospect

I The Decline of Neo-Kantianism

THE neo-Kantian tradition made its great contribution to philosophy on the heels of the enormous expansion of scientific knowledge that was occurring in the mid- to late-nineteenth century. This school, centered in Marburg, took as one of its primary tasks to investigate the structure and implications of scientific theory for our understanding of human knowledge. And though their efforts were rooted in the perspectives of Immanuel Kant, they were not the mere servile extrapolators of Kant's views in the new historical contexts. Rather, they linked their perspective to what they considered Kant's profound insight into the forms of knowledge, science, ethics, art, what we essentially consider the phenomenology of thought. We cannot know reality through the means of science. Nor can we ever reduce science to an ontological core of sensory experiences. Over and over again, we hear that the search is for the law or the logic that gives rise to knowledge. It is not for the substantive origins of the real world.

This relatively instrumentalist approach, which culminated in Cassirer's writings on the structure of scientific knowledge, has been upheld since. It is a rare scientist who today speaks of the "advance of knowledge on the ever expanding boundaries of objectivity."[1] Even the dream of an orthodox logical model that would allow man his special reportorial role of spectator and analyzer is no longer possible. Man now gets in the way of experimental and thus theoretical objectivity. Science is a structure of symbolically organized experience with a unique logic of development that is almost impossible to determine or predict in advance. It seems to rise more freely and creatively with fewer conceptual fetters as it is increasingly absorbed into abstract mathematical forms. It tends toward universal implication, and where it is restricted from this tendency by indigestible counter examples, as was Newtonian mechanics by electromagnetic theory, it searches for new conceptual invariants, so that it might vault once more toward its goal of absorbing all experience in a set of lean, abstract, and nonimagistic principles.

In claiming for itself no unique metaphysical privileges, scientific knowledge thus opened the door to that very obvious second stage of study in which Cassirer was quick to engage, the study of cultural symbolism. There are here two motivating factors that shaped Cassirer's orientation. One is the basic theoretical concern for an understanding of the structure of cultural thought, language, myth, religion, and art. Common sense tells us that these domains have their legitimate status in culture. Their use does not necessarily turn individuals away from reason. And they are certainly complementing aspects of the human spirit as compared with science. Now that Cassirer understood that these domains could never be absorbed and reduced by science and that they were not aberrant and wayward, he could plunge into an unconditional examination of their "inner laws of development and function."

A second interest is Cassirer's keen appreciation and sensitivity to the great cultural achievements of the West, indeed of civilized man in general. This is reflected in the steady outpouring of works on a variety of philosophers, poets, aestheticians, and scientists. The creative act and the innovative power of the human mind offered itself as a harmonious fascination, an important adjunct to Cassirer's systematic studies. If a logical structure is to be apprehended in the various symbolic forms of cultural expression, it has not been placed there by some supranatural force. Rational and creative man carved out those achievements. And man has done so by mining the potentialities that lie within him. The social environment may have assisted humans, thus Cassirer's concern with Western civilization as a context. But it is the multifarious work of so many powerful and insistent minds that has created and moved Western civilization to the position of domination at the beginning of the twentieth century.

The following through of the theory of symbolic forms to its logical conclusions brought forth some new and unexpected facts. The logic that leads upward in conceptual and creative richness in the arts, religion, and science, which creates new areas of knowledge in history, mathematics, and logic, also leads back down toward certain root problems. Here, we see that the process of symbolic conception is preceded by a more basic level of symbolic intention, the process of symbolic pregnance, where the raw materials of experience coalesce into totalities of meaning. Whether it is perceptual experience or linguistic expression, or even the emotional, expressive awareness of power or significance, the symbolic act is a creative, productive act. It carves out meaning from the inchoateness of life. The world is not given to us as such; it must be discovered by creating intentional boundaries and connecting these boundaries of signification with each other. Thus is born the fabric of cultural meaning.

But from where does this propensity issue? What is its significance, character, or context? Here, Cassirer was forced to go further. The basic human predisposition to envisage experience in terms of form and structure could be understood by contrasting it with human behavior that was limited, or severed from its wholeness, as in aphasic disabilities or in comparison with animal behavior. The concept *animal symbolicum* came to have an overriding meaning in the structure of symbolic forms. In this philosophical form, as a philosophical anthropology contrasting cultural behavior with the more organic drives in animals, Cassirer's work exerted a fascination for English-speaking readers as compared with his earlier, more logical and epistemological studies of the structure of thought and of the various cognitive disciplines of civilized man.

One could say that Cassirer had given us a "macroscope" by which we could envision the logical possibilities of culture. In an era increasingly beset by social and political instabilities, the self-confidence that derived from this curiosity in the achievement and structure of the forms of knowledge was now seen as an anachronistic remainder of a more self-assured time. From all sides, the sense of *Angst*, despair, and futility that beset the individual in the urban context was matched by an increasing suspicion of Western civilization, of high culture. Not merely was culture compromised if we saw it as a product of psychic sublimation or class-induced power, but it was hated for its reflection of a world where social exploitation was an assumed condition of things. Ultimately, as in our own day, even the rationalism that had created science and technology and this powerful middle-class majority would be challenged as cause for the environmental blight, both psychic and material, that had spread over our world.

Thus it is that neo-Kantianism, of all the twentieth-century philosophies, has faded most rapidly from the scene. Alone, of all the recent philosophical traditions, it seemed to have less to say to the new generations. True, the convulsion that overtook Europe in World War II wreaked havoc on the intellectual homeland of this tradition. But this affliction had the same physical impact on the other Continental traditions.

One explanation is that Cassirer raised, as part of his researches, too many issues of scientific fact and theory. His empirical approach lent itself to the more specific inquiries of a host of different research theoreticians. People like Kurt Goldstein, Heinz Werner, Susanne Langer, and Noam Chomsky were, consciously or not, working in the heartland of the Kantian philosophical anthropology. Yet, their work, while enormously influential, did not come together to form a school of thought as such. As the world turned away in concern over the pressing issues of survival, Cassirer, evicted from his own beloved homeland, was also denied a necessary succession.

II *Philosophical Relevance*

Let us pursue this issue of philosophical relevancy. It is at the heart of criticism most often leveled at Cassirer. The charge is not easily answered. Its accuracy depends on two problematic factors. One is the obvious one of relevancy for whom and for what era. Obviously, certain philosophers, relevant for their own period and perhaps shortly afterward, have not stood the long-term test. And just as obviously, other thinkers, while perhaps having varied impact over the long haul, are still seriously read and considered. Their relevance has been established through clear, time-tested historical and philosophical criteria.

The other aspect of relevancy depends upon the criteria to be utilized. Certainly, Cassirer and the neo-Kantian movement loosed a number of seminal perspectives into the intellectual life of the West. From Albert Einstein to Henry Margenau, from the Gestalt psychologists to Piaget and the psycholinguistic movement, from Georg Simmel to Levi-Strauss, there is work in practically all the disciplines that reflects the revivification of Kant which the Marburg school as early as the late nineteenth century had effected.

Many speak in terms of the macroscopic perspectives of Cassirer, of his lack of attention to the specific and poignant concerns that one finds in phenomenology, existentialism, and even the religious philosophies. Much of the depth of these new traditions can be seen as a substitute for the more traditional dogmatic concerns of the past. It can be said that in an era wherein the confident, dynamic optimism of traditional society had been shaken, other philosophies came to give greater sustenance to the individual. Whether they were secular, metaphysical, or religious, these philosophies helped individuals to affirm their sense of location; they put the individual in a context of real decision making without superimposing upon him larger cultural destinies and processes that were indifferent to his real situation.

Of course, the solution to this problem cannot be found in the momentary consensus by which one philosophy is able to exploit its claims, attract adherents, and attain positions of power whereby its virtues can be trumpeted without contest. The test of a philosophy is how truthful it is in terms of the long-term interests of man and as a guide to thought as well as action. Even in that basic question of perspectives, whether we use the macroscope or the microscope, the problematic issue is whether human experience is clarified by the particular method. And the question can never be an issue of the historic moment. For, certainly, it may be that existentialism helps to stabilize one's perspectives on the world under certain historical situations. But will it meet the test in a variety of situations? Will history confirm its perspectives in the long run?

As early as 1929, it was clear that neo-Kantianism's influence was on the wane. English philosophy remained fixed in its positivistic concerns. America was firmly in the hands of the pragmatists. And in Germany, phenomenology was advancing steadily. Marburg was already in the camp of this latter group of philosophers. In that year, Cassirer and Heidegger met at Davos to debate their divergent views on the philosophy of Kant. But it was more than an intellectual joust; it reflected the confrontation of two very different outlooks on life, each with its own sense of truth and relevance and its own vision of man and knowledge.

Hendrik Pos, a friend of Cassirer, was an observer at that event and reported on it from his own not disinterested position. But, as the reader will shortly note, it was the subsequent events that lent additional historic credence to Pos' views. Had history gone a bit differently, it would have been related to succeeding generations of philosophy students in antoher way.

Heidegger spoke of a Kant who was concerned to delineate the finitude of man. This limitation explained man's orientation toward the transcendent experience. Cassirer saw this finitude as the starting point for man's liberation through his own powers rather than as the search for a suprahuman reality. To Pos, the difference between the two men was not merely an intellectual difference; rather the intellectual difference seemed to reflect a deeper contrast in larger human perspectives:

Here stood, on the one side, the representative of the best in the universalistic traditions of German culture, a man for whom Idealism was the victorious power which is called to mold and spiritualize human life. This man, the heir of Kant, stood there tall, powerful, and serene. His effect upon his audience lay in his mastery of exposition, in the Apollonian element. From the beginning he had within him the liberal culture of Central Europe, the product of a long tradition. In both spiritual lineaments and external appearance, this man belonged to the epoch of Kant, of Goethe, and of Kleist....[2]

Of Heidegger, Pos represents a picture of a man of different background, outlook, and emotional constitution:

As a man, however, he was completely different. Of *"petit bourgeoisie"* descent from southwest Germany, he had never lost his accent. In him this was readily forgiven, being taken as a mark of firm-rootedness and peasant genuineness.... At home as almost no one else in Aristotle and the scholastics, in Kant and Hegel, he constructed for himself a philosophy which, on the side of method, came close to the phenomenology of his teacher, Husserl. In point of content, however, this philosophy was of course entirely his own: there lay feelings at the base of it which were concealed by the gigantic intellectual superstructure. But when one listened to his lectures, listened to this gloomy, somewhat whining and apprehensive tone of voice, then there flowed forth the feelings which this man harbored or at least which he knew how to awaken. These were feelings of loneliness, of oppression, and of frustration, such as one has in anxious dreams, but now present in a clear and wakeful state of mind.[3]

Pos contrasts the tenor of the debate — the attitude of negativism and finitude on the one hand and the optimism and hopefulness of Cassirer on the other. As for Heidegger, Pos calls him, "The little man with the sinister willful speech, who was at home with these morose feelings, who loved to say that philosophy is no

fun, the despiser of Goethe — (this man) over against the representative of Enlightenment, basking in spiritual fortune, for whom
the philosopher's life was joy and inspiration, and who in Goethe
paid homage to the universal man." Pos goes on to say:

> The whole discussion was the intuitive representation of this profound
> cleavage between the two men. The one abrupt, negative, his attitude one
> of protest; the other kindly, gracious, accommodating, always concerned
> to give his partner more honor than he deserved.... The conclusion was
> not without human symbolism; the magnanimous man offered his hand to
> his opponent: but it was not accepted.[4]

These events occurred in 1929. Cassirer was at that time Rector
of the University of Hamburg and Heidegger a member of the Marburg University philosophy faculty. Four years later, in 1933,
Cassirer was out at Hamburg and on his way to England, a refugee
from the Nazis. At the same time, Heidegger was appointed Rector
of Freiberg University. In his inaugural address at Freiberg,
Heidegger "professed himself unreservedly for National
Socialism."[5]
We cannot take these events as symptomatic of the inevitable
direction that any one philosophy must take. Many fine thinkers
who were phenomenologists or existentialists opposed fascism and
suffered mightily for their opposition. What Pos seems to imply in
this comparison of Cassirer and Heidegger, in comments written
shortly after the former's death in 1945, was that the expulsion and
wandering of Cassirer in search of refuge and the blind commitment of Heidegger to Nazism symbolized the destruction of the
European philosophical tradition.
When we look beyond the more limited decline in the neo-
Kantian and phenomenological traditions since World War II, we
must inevitably take into account the changing role of philosophy
in this social and cultural milieu. A truer evaluation and understanding of Cassirer's contribution can only be formed if one
examines not merely the competitive status of the various
philosophies but also their relationship to the historical circumstances then existing.

III   *In the Perspective of Time*

One can better assess the message of Cassirer's neo-Kantianism if
one understands the relationship of its impact on the intellectual as

well as the social conditions of the late twentieth century to the need for a more general philosophical reconstruction. For the most part, the great philosophical positions that had significant impact on the perceptions and lives of the makers of our world were created in the late nineteenth century. With the exception of the positivistic tradition — both in its Continental (Vienna circle) and English (language analysis) form — which has its roots in the writings of Ernst Mach and John Stuart Mill, our conceptual world was created almost a century ago.

Much has occurred technologically and socially in the intervening decades to transmute these philosophies into forms which their makers would hardly recognize. In fact, lucky are those philosophical traditions that have not been appropriated by followers subservient to the dynamics of contemporary social events. And, while the surrender of Heidegger to Hitler is only an extreme example, other events reflect the sad state of independent creative work philosophically significant for modern man.

For example, while much in Marxism is powerfully suggestive of the condition of man valid at all times in the historical dialectic, independent philosophical amplifications have been hindered by the political expropriations of Marxist philosophy by the Stalinist and Maoist ideologies. One can only point to the brief if suggestive renaissance in Czechoslovakia in 1968, which was brutally extinguished by the tanks of the Soviet Union.

Again, one can argue that Freudianism, if not in the strictest sense a philosophical movement, was certainly one of the most powerful intellectual systems of thought that came out of the last century. Not only did it generate a great deal of conceptual debate and numerous submovements, but it also gave good opportunity for empirical investigation and experimentation. Unfortunately, by the mid-twentieth century, much of its theoretical vitality was vitiated when it became absorbed by a tradition in therapy that had a unique sociocultural ambience. Most delicately put, the movement in therapy seemed to become an adjunct of our affluent culture in catering to the personal and psychological difficulties of the professional and managerial classes. Indeed, Freud's work had been experimentally shaped through his treatment of middle-class Viennese at the turn of the century. But his more general writings argued for a universal application of his theories to the condition of human kind in general.

One wonders whether the limited applications of both Marxism and Freudianism have precluded intellectual criticism that would have stimulated a more flexible adaptation of these ideas. On the other hand, it is a rare philosophy that speaks to man at any one moment in history, and given popular acclaim, which at the same time can resist the inevitable encrustations of institutionalism. The possibilities that inhere in any philosophy perhaps can only be rediscovered at some distance, when the immediate followers and their institutional embodiment have weakened and more flexible possibilities consequently have been exposed.

The example of Aristotle and his rediscovery by the medieval scholars in the twelfth and thirteenth centuries is one example. The rediscovery of Plato and Pythagoras by the scholars of the sixteenth and seventeenth centuries is but another. It is interesting that in our own time the enthusiastic followers of John Dewey in education and social philosophy inevitably gave rise to their own antitheses. And while Dewey's instrumentalism never became a national philosophy, it had certain conformist tendencies that blinded both critics and followers to the latent conceptual possibilities of this position.

Morton White, writing in the immediate aftermath of this tradition, criticized its involvement with the method of instrumental thought and lack of involvement with more tangible policy embodiments. These would have clarified some of the educational or even political policies that Dewey's followers proposed.[6] A generation later, White could write that his criticisms were premature. In the time since, much ideological demagoguery has taken place, stemming from a variety of intellectual sources. Indeed, a philosopher stressing the restraining role of scientific method in thought and action and the necessity of being disciplined by the evidence at hand and at all points, is still an essential need in our own day. Dewey's message is even more relevant now than when he first set it forth as a variant of the original pragmatic movement of Charles S. Peirce, William James, and George H. Mead.

That most optimistic and typically American philosophical movement has also run its course. Time had passed its message into context and thence into the memory of textbooks in the history of philosophy. Our world is very different, and it will no doubt necessitate a certain distancing from the present preoccupations with environmental and political survival and with the social distribution and redistribution of the wealth of technology to bring about a more openly reflective era. The battle between reason and myth noted by Cassirer in *The Myth of the State* and the struggle between Eros and Thanatos that Freud warned us about are still in process. And no matter how partisan one is to any particular philosophical position, the fact that ideologies prosper and the din of propaganda continues the corruption of reason into a steady escalation of violence, war, and terrorism, all point to an inevitably degrading impact on philosophical discourse. Thus, one cannot reasonably discuss the vision of hope and the quest for a knowledge of man and culture inherent in Cassirer's neo-Kantianism, unless one speaks about a set of human conditions that is yet to come, toward which the implicit commitments of a Cassirer might lead us.

IV *A Challenge for Cultural Reform*

The world was in ascent when Cassirer was first beginning his researches on the nature of knowledge, culture, and, eventually, man. Even World War I, which disturbed him deeply, did not affect that intellectual optimism that thrust him into the writing of the philosophy of symbolic forms. The power of science, the enormous social transformations that technology had unlocked, plus the possibilities for social advancement for the energetic from all levels of society, were aspects of this optimism. To the universal revelations of successive scientific revolutions was added the enormous cultural fertility of the West, which science and technology seemed not to have disturbed. Overall, this was an era that revealed the constructive power of man, his external as well as internal resources and skills.

This picture of man and the possibilities of cultural life was part of a three-hundred year tradition in Europe, in which reason and creativity had taken the center stage. A new era in Western life has arrived which has seen the overwhelming growth of machinelike institutions of government and industry, whose main preoccupation is servicing the material needs of mass societies and feeding them a steady barrage of propagandistic myths and fairy tales to keep them surfeited and content. One can only now see how far we have departed from the confident rationalistic orientation of the past. Cassirer's researches into the structure of mythological thinking, the subsequent work of Carl Jung, Robert Graves, and Joseph Campbell in making us aware of those powerful emotional concerns that lie below the surface of ordinary experience, give us a tentative awareness that this residuum of the arational is there and can be appropriated by any powerful group for its own insidious manipulations.

We are aware, after Hitler, and now after Stalin and Mao, that the secular rationality of man is a slender reed. The struggle against religious dogmatism to achieve science — to banish astrology, phlogiston, and alchemy — was not the historical rubicon that we thought it would be. John Dewey, whose instrumentalist views on the nature of knowledge parallel Cassirer's, devoted his life to the method of pragmatism, to show that when certain ideas could not be subsumed to scientific discourse, they were meaningless. But, as Cassirer has pointed out, these meaningless concepts, which are empty shells of words when considered from the standpoint of scientific actuality, can be sanctioned by man's will. In a sense, mythic ideas are impervious to the logic of science if man wills to believe.

Today, our life is permeated by a variety of "reason bending" institutions ranging from comparatively innocuous advertising and the "packaging" of political candidates, the clever use of mass media to condition the people to accept certain stylistic social trends, to the more frightening scenarios perpetrated on the masses in Red Square. How delicate is the flower of scientific and philosophical sobriety. And how easy it is to manipulate the thinly veneered experience for decision making in the people. The world seems to have transformed itself into several vast totalitarian machines that vie for power with each other while at the same time they need to manipulate its restive populations so that they acquiesce to the machines' survivalistic needs.

It is true that power politics and social injustices existed during the generations of the ascent of Europe and the West. Yet the diversity of these societies and the inability of even great despotisms such as Napoleonic France or Czarist Russia to penetrate the fabric of culture seems to have been the saving grace. The plurality of freedoms, scientific, philosophical, artistic, and religious, allowed the helter-skelter changes seen in the face of society. This richness and openness is no longer evident. Inexorable material and social needs seem to be determining the policy actions of the ruling cliques of our day. The propaganda machines, using all the media of our interconnected world, grind out the necessary messages, eliciting the appropriate responses.

Can we return to a vision of knowledge, culture, and man in

which freedom to explore the varied strands of fact and theory leads to new cultural vistas, unconditioned by existing institutional powers? Can we provide a social environment whereby the unlimited creative powers of man can be loosed as indiscriminately and unselfconsciously as they were in the past? Cassirer's deep involvement with the creative function of thought thus has a deep relevance in an era that cannot allow itself the openness, privacy, and indeterminacy that undergirded the rise of Western culture. What if the Communist party were disowned; what if General Motors or I.B.M. dissolved; where will the jobs be; how can we allow people the luxury of a world of creative thought when four billion people must be fed each day? In a few years, it will be seven or eight billion.

From the standpoint of neo-Kantianism, the great problem of our era is the generation of reason in the confrontation with the realities of our current social dynamics. The set of social conditions we now confront provides a need and opportunity for a new symbolic form. One might say that the development of culture in its highest and richest sense reflects an unevenness in the development of mankind in general. The intellectual and aesthetic development in Europe from the Renaissance on was grafted onto a simple, unsophisticated society. The technological fallout from science has been precipitous and has not allowed us to develop the social understanding necessary to control all these forces.

The result has been the disintegration of confidence in the power of reason. This has followed upon the cauterization of the normally optimistic and rational philosophies, both neo-Kantian and pragmatic, and the domination by the pessimism and determinism inherent in existentialism, dogmatic Marxism, and Freudianism. Other philosophical movements have moved away from a concern with man and culture to more ontological and religious concerns, or as with academic philosophies, with linguistic and logical issues of a specialized and professional nature.

The return to the philosophical confrontation of cultural and social issues is a more difficult requirement. In the pragmatic tradition of John Dewey it was expected that the instrumental method could apply itself to short-term problems, what Karl Popper once called piecemeal engineering. But, of course, this is part of our present dilemma. Many actions that seemed to be wise and rational in solving the contextual issues of the day have turned out to be disastrous over the course of a generation. One can merely cite the commitment to the automobile or the mass extension of medical technology to underdeveloped peoples, which has decreased death rates without giving them the ability to control birth rates.

The Deweyan tradition, however, was concerned with the problem of cultivating intelligence through education and social policy. And in this sense, it has a stronger activist role to play in shaping the popular attitude toward instrumental solutions. Cassirer saw this thrust for rational understanding as part of the natural process of the maturation of civilization. He had not been prepared for the massive intervention of social discordancy. It was important for him to note finally and attempt to confront the meaning for man and culture of mythical thinking. He perceived how close it is to the surface and how it must be forever fought and neutralized. Freud understood the extent to which deep-seated and destructive dynamics went to the heart of human nature. And he was pessimistic. Dewey was more typically an American optimist. In directing his analytical method at the traditional and historical dogmas of orthodox religion, he thought that unreason could be penetrated and dissolved by method.

Freud and the later Cassirer were probably more realistic. In placing myth at the very origins of human thought, Cassirer first recognized its presence. By placing it in antithesis to the forces of reason, contending for dominance over man's cultural life, he alerted us to the necessity of avoiding complacency, of preparing for a long and perhaps never-to-be-completed struggle. There is almost a touch of the gnostic in Cassirer's last passage in *The Myth of the State* when he contrasts the forces of darkness, which must be periodically subjugated by the forces of light if we are to hope to realize our peculiarly human powers for creativity.[7]

There is, however, an important mitigating factor in Cassirer's noninstrumental intellectual and historical approach to the study of knowledge, culture, and human nature. He may not have proposed a method of thought, as did Dewey, or a method of therapy, as did Freud. There is, however, a vision of man and culture toward which we can direct our efforts. It is not enough to propose a war against social irrationalities. We cannot pack myth back into its appropriate ceremonial, poetic, and aesthetic domain unless we can infuse a rationality of fact and experiment, an openness to theory. We must also have the flexibility to abandon less successful postulations for new hypotheses and ultimately to offer long range goals that are consonant with the most universal conceptions of man and society.

There is thus a utopian element in Cassirer's philosophy that has latent power even at this distance. Cassirer's concern with the infinite possibilities in man rather than man's finite limitations is today more than ever an important and powerful element in his philosophy that calls for more study and amplification. This need for the utopian element in our vision of man and society is testified to by the powerful attractiveness of Marxism. But Marxism leads us to the door of the good life and rarely shows us what it tangibly can be. So many have been cheated by totalitarian societies that have seduced men by persuading them of a utopian vision to come. In reality they have merely provided a revolutionary method by which one set of oppressors has been dialectically substituted for the next.

Marxism's criterion of a structure of society whereby each man shall work to exemplify the saying, "from each according to his ability to each according to his need" is thus a bare schematic outline without flesh; it does not show us how to recognize the image for the real things. There is no sense here of man's needs deeper than his material relationships. Certainly Marx meant that there was more to man than this. Yet his nonexploitative society avoids the specifics, indeed the content, of man's life. We can argue with this superstructure of nonexploitation and the respect for the work and efforts of each person. But in the hands of totalitarians there is precious little in Marxism to allow us to do battle in the name of a Marxian view of human nature that demands the spiritual freedom of man to create and think. There is as yet no Marxism in which the barriers and walls of state power really wither away to allow man to develop in cultural and social contexts appropriate to his "infinite" potentialities.

And this is exactly what neo-Kantianism points to. The view of human nature as *animal symbolicum* at which Cassirer arrived is not a position that argues for an elite culture. His concern for the intellectual and aesthetic achievements of our most profound individuals sets them in the context of a broader conception of man. This view shows the universal participation of all human beings in the circle of symbolic activity. The growth of civilizations can be understood best in the context of this powerful human drive for the symbolic recreation of experience. The meaning of culture and the symbolic drives that gave rise to culture cannot be found in any theory of materialistic causation or in any view of man determined by anterior drives. The revolutionary character of this view is that, in spite of all the materialistic and economic preoccupations in which shallow societies attempt to envelop their citizens, man's nature is forcibly revealed in his striving to go beyond the material and economic, even beyond the gadgetry of our own American culture.

The inner symbolic drive for meaning is a creative, limitless process; it has no end. It is stimulated by the very contexts of human social experience. But it does not depend upon external circumstances to do its work. Otherwise, man would never have climbed out of the cave. The hope then is that no matter what the present circumstances are, the drive for universality in reason, to see relationships, to test ideas in the crucible of experience, and to set them into wider and wider circles of experience will continue. Man must aim beyond his immediate circumference; he must envision more ideal and abstract symbolic constructs.

The argument is not that this trend in man toward the creative dissolution of any contemporary intellectual constructs will necessarily occur. It is that it is an immanent trend in human nature that, given half a chance, sociopolitically will manifest itself. History demonstrates this fact. What is even more interesting is that though Cassirer envisions an almost infinite panorama of universally oriented scientific structures in a variety of disciplines, supplementing each other without end, their insights are open to the assent and criticism of all mankind. As he once put it, thought is universal.

But beyond the scientific and even philosophical claims of universality is that vast realm of the nondiscursive, which his follower Susanne Langer has explored in much detail, that area of ritual, rite, religion, and above all art.[8] In the various arts we see the most multifaceted exemplification of man's symbolic nature. In every dimension of experience, from poetry to architecture, song and the dance, the aesthetic sense finds its own possibilities. No rock, flower, or taste is exempt from the aesthetic transformation that man imposes. It is a universal drive, to play with sense, feeling, and thought, to turn into a creative insight what never existed before. Here we see exhibited man's infinite possibilities for recreation, and not merely in the historical or chronological sense of supplanting that which has gone before. In art, the competition is not for one view of truth or social reality. Every aesthetic contribution takes its place beside others, to compete, it is true, for the respect and appreciation of the public for the genuine insights and virtues it offers. Its metaphysical claims are for a diversity of realities, successive truths, or truths standing side by side, but never limited by a fixed canon of what is to be seen as real, permanent, or beautiful.

In this sense, art is pluralistic. Like the languages of the world, each capable of its unique poetry, drama, fiction, and each standing as a distinct and unique contribution to the vision of what man is and what he can do, the arts are significant agents of change in a culture.[9] One might argue that cultures change through material and technological succession or through political development. But in a far deeper sense, a Goethe, Shakespeare, Pushkin, Cervantes has altered our linguistic sensitivities and possibilities as no mere material alteration could. But, it can work the other way. Can it be doubted that "Nazi-Deutsch" and "T.V. English" have debased their respective cultures in a far more significant way than the mere political or economic arrangements that they reflect, would signify?

Thus in the diversity of cultural possibilities as well as in the universality inherent in the various sciences and philosophies, there is a vision of man that allows for complete indeterminacy. The inherent freedom of man will be fulfilled in this future society when his social and material conditions will allow for the true exploitation of his creative depths. The surging power of the mind, the drive for symbolic envisagement can go both ways. Limited, fettered by paralyzing social conditions, it can be degraded and caricatured, a modern recreation of the atavistic remnants of the mythic level of existence. Given the opportunity, as it has in the past, all human beings, by contrast, can participate variously in the richness, diversity, and openness that are inherent in the cultures of man.

Cassirer was not able to show us the way out of a world that had split apart and fallen in wreckage about us. The conditions of humanity have not appreciably improved in the years since his death. He did not in his philosophy devise a method or offer a program that would set us on a proper political or economic course. That will have to come from a different sort of philosophical perspective.

But he did show us what the nature of human knowledge is, and how it reflects the deepest motivations of our cultural existence. He gave us a glimpse of that powerful generation of symbolic meanings that inheres in the mystery of man. Finally, his view of knowledge and culture emphasized its creative possibilities and the self-fulfilling need of man for these kinds of symbol mongering. As such, Cassirer's philosophy is one of hope, a vision of a mundane utopia, that can be realized in the simple capacity of man to do what he loves to do.

Notes and References

Chapter Two

1. A. C. Ewing, *A Short Commentary on Kant's Critique of Pure Reason* (Chicago: University of Chicago Press, 1938), p. 12.
2. "Kant," in *Encyclopedia of the Social Sciences* (New York: Macmillan, 1932), p. 540.
3. For Liebermann, Lange, and other neo-Kantians, see Lewis White Beck, "Neo-Kantianism," in *Encyclopedia of Philosophy* (New York: Macmillan, 1967), pp. 468–73.
4. Beck (ibid.) quotes from Lange's *History of Materialism,* III, 342, 347.
5. Cassirer, "Neo-Kantianism," in *Encyclopedia Britannica,* 14th ed. (New York, 1928), p. 215.
6. See Julius Ebbinghaus, "Hermann Cohen," in *Encyclopedia of Philosophy,* pp. 125–28.
7. Quoted by Cassirer in "Hermann Cohen 1842–1918," *Social Research* 10 (1943), 224.
8. See Mariano Campo, "Paul Natorp," in *Encyclopedia of Philosophy,* pp. 445–48.
9. Beck, "Neo-Kantianism," p. 471.
10. Cassirer, *The Philosophy of Symbolic Forms,* trans. Ralph Manheim (New Haven: Yale University Press, 1953–1957), III, 52. Henceforth abbreviated *PSF.*
11. Toni Cassirer, "Aus meinem Leben mit Ernst Cassirer" (New York, 1950, mimeo) p. 77.
12. "Neo-Kantianism," p. 216.

Chapter Three

1. "Ernst Cassirer," in *The Philosophy of Ernst Cassirer,* ed. Paul Arthur Schilpp (New York: Tudor Publishing Co., 1949), p. 43.
2. Marburg, N.G. Elwert, 1902.
3. "Newton and Leibniz," *Philosophical Review* 52 (1943), p. 385.
4. Cassirer, "Newton and Leibzig", pp. 387–88.
5. Toni Cassirer, "Aus meinem Leben mit Ernst Cassirer, p. 76.
6. Felix Kaufmann, "Cassirer's Theory of Scientific Knowledge," in *The Philosophy of Ernst Cassirer,* p. 187.

186   ERNST CASSIRER

7. Cassirer, *Determinism and Indeterminism in Modern Physics,* trans. O.T. Benfey (New Haven: Yale University Press, 1956), p. 130.

8. *PSF,* I, 168.

9. Ernst Mach, "The Economical Nature of Physics," in *Popular Science Lectures,* trans. Thomas J. McCormack (Lasalle, Ill.: Open Court, 1943), pp. 208-9.

10. Pierre Duhem, *The Aim and Structure of Physical Theory,* trans. Philip Wiener (Princeton: Princeton University Press, 1954), pp. 333-35.

11. Emile Meyerson, *Identity and Reality,* trans. Kate Lowenberg (London: Allen & Unwin, 1930).

12. Kaufman, "Cassirer's Theory of Scientific Knowledge," in Schilpp, *The Philosophy of Ernst Cassirer,* p. 190.

13. Cassirer, *Substance and Function,* trans. W.C. and M.C. Swabey (New York: Dover, 1953), pp. 307-8.

14. Gawronsky, "Cassirer's Contribution to the Epistemology of Physics," in Schilpp, *The Philosophy of Ernst Cassirer,* p. 224.

15. Kant, *Neuen Lehrbegriff der Bewegung und der Ruhe,* in Cassirer, *Einstein's Theory of Relativity*, trans. W.C. and M.C. Swabey (New York: Dover, 1953), p. 410.

16. Kant, *Metaphysischen Anfangsgrunden der Naturwissenschaft,* in Cassirer, *Einstein's Theory of Relativity,* p. 416.

17. Cassirer, *Einstein's Theory of Relativity,* p. 421.

18. *Relativity: The Special and General Theory* (Chicago: H. Regnery, 1951), p. 37.

19. *PSF,* III, 459.

20. Ibid., p. 472.

21. "Introduction," in *Physics and Philosophy,* by Werner Heisenberg (New York: Harper and Row, 1958), p. 7.

22. Ibid., p. 8.

23. Cassirer, *Determinism and Indeterminism in Modern Physics,* pp. 191-93.

24. Ibid., p. 194.

25. *The Problem of Knowledge,* trans. W.H. Woglom and C.W. Hendel (New Haven: Yale University Press, 1950), pp. 110-11.

26. Northrop, "Introduction," in *Physics and Philosophy,* p. 17.

27. Cassirer, *Determinism and Indeterminism in Modern Physics,* p. 193.

28. *PSF,* III, 378.

29. Ibid., p. 377.

30. Stephen Barker, *The Philosophy of Mathematics* (New York: Prentice Hall, 1964), pp. 74-75.

31. *PSF,* III, 381.

32. Ibid., pp. 379-80.

33. Ibid., pp. 381-82.

34. Ibid., p. 386.

35. Barker, *The Philosophy of Mathematics,* pp. 96–97.
36. Ibid., p. 97.
37. *PSF,* III, 385.
38. Ibid., p. 387.
39. Ibid., p. 398.
40. Ibid., p. 404.

Chapter Four

1. *PSF,* I, 78.
2. "Introduction," *PSF,* III, ix.
3. *PSF,* III, 121.
4. *Language and Myth,* trans. Susanne Langer (New York: Dover, 1946), pp. 15–16.
5. Ibid., p. 43.
6. *PSF,* I, 206.
7. Ibid., pp. 213–14.
8. Ibid., p. 223.
9. Ibid., pp. 223–24.
10. Ibid., p. 228.
11. Ibid., p. 239.
12. Ibid., pp. 247–48.
13. Ibid., p. 292.
14. Cited in ibid., p. 291.
15. Ibid. , I, Chapter 4: "Language as Expression of Conceptual Thought" and "Concept and Class Formation in Language"; and especially, ibid., Chapter 5: "Language and the Expression of the Forms of Pure Relation" and "The Sphere of Judgment and the Concept of Relation." These are important and tantalizing sections, summits of Cassirer's enquiry into language.
16. *PSF,* I, 306.
17. Ibid., p. 310.
18. Ibid., pp. 308–9.
19. Ibid., p. 310.
20. Ibid., p. 311–13.
21. Ibid., p. 294.
22. Ibid., p. 319.
23. Ibid., III, 51–57.
24. Ibid., p. 57.
25. Ibid.
26. Ibid., I, 294.
27. Ibid., III, 64–66.
28. Ibid., pp. 76–77.
29. Ibid., p. 90.
30. Ibid., p. 91.

31. Ibid., II, 200.
32. Ibid., p. 110.
33. Ibid., p. 151.
34. Ibid., pp. 217–18.
35. Ibid., p. 239.
36. Ibid., p. 235.
37. Ibid., p. 236.
38. Ibid.
39. Ibid., pp. 237–38; see also *Language and Myth,* Chapter 5.
40. *An Essay On Man* (New Haven: Yale University Press, 1944), p. 98.
41. Ibid., p. 107.
42. After writing *The Philosophy of the Enlightenment* (1932) and *Determinism and Indeterminism in Modern Physics* (1936).
43. *The Myth of the State* (New York: Doubleday, 1955), p. 351. See Walter Laqueur, *Weimar: a cultural history* (London: Weidenfeld and Nicolson, 1974); also Peter Gay, *Weimar Culture: The Outsider as Insider* (New York: Harper and Row, 1968).
44. *The Myth of the State,* p. 356.
45. Ibid., p. 357.
46. Ibid., p. 360.
47. Ibid., Chapter 3, especially p. 43.
48. "On Cassirer's Theory of Language and Myth," in Schilpp, pp. 379–400.
49. Ibid., p. 398.
50. *The Myth of the State,* p. 375.
51. *Language and Myth,* p. 98.
52. "Cassirer's Placement of Art," in Schilpp, pp. 605–30.
53. "Ernst Cassirer's Functional Approach to Art and Literature," in Schilpp, *The Philosophy of Ernst Cassirer,* pp. 631-59.
54. *Language and Myth,* p. 98.
55. Ibid.
56. *PSF,* II, 260.
57. Ibid., p. 261.
58. *An Essay On Man,* pp. 143–44.
59. Ibid., p. 158.
60. Ibid., p. 154.
61. *PSF,* II, 261.
62. "Das Symbolproblem und seine Stellung im System der Philosophie," *Zeitschrift für Ästhetik und Allgemeine Kunstwissenschaft* 21 (1927) 296, cited in Gilbert, "Cassirer's Placement of Art," in Schilpp, *The Philosophy of Ernst Cassirer,* p. 609.
63. *The Logic of the Humanities,* trans. C.S. Howe (New Haven: Yale University Press, 1961), pp. 84–85.
64. *An Essay On Man,* p. 160.

65. "Ernst Cassirer's Functional Approach to Art and Literature," in *The Philosophy of Ernst Cassirer,* in Schilpp, pp. 656-57.

66. *An Essay On Man,* p. 175.

67. Ibid., p. 186.

68. Ibid., pp. 176-77.

69. All from *An Essay On Man.*

70. Cassirer, *The Problem of Knowledge,* pp. 308-24.

71. See Rudolf Carnap, "Testability and Meaning" in *Readings in the Philosophy of Science,* ed. H. Feigl and M. Brodbeck (New York: 1953), especially pp. 69-70.

Chapter Five

1. *PSF,* III, 228; see also Ibid., I, 186-97.

2. See Ibid., III, 209-15.

3. Ibid., pp. 96-99, 196-200.

4. Ibid., pp. 202-3.

5. Ibid., p. 203.

6. Ibid., p. 116.

7. Ibid., p. 215.

8. Hughlings Jackson, in *PSF,* III, 213.

9. Henry Head, in *PSF,* III, 214-15.

10. Adhemar Gelb and Kurt Goldstein, in *PSF,* III, 228.

11. *PSF,* III, 238-39.

12. Ibid., p. 271.

13. Ibid., p. 274.

14. Ibid., pp. 275-276.

15. Ibid., p. 277.

16. *An Essay On Man,* p. 70.

17. Ibid., p. 68.

18. Langer, "On Cassirer's Theory of Language and Myth," in Schilpp, pp. 396-98.

19. John Dewey, quoted in Cassirer, *An Essay on Man,* p. 67; also p. 78.

20. Kurt Goldstein and M. Scheerer, "Abstract and Concrete Behavior," *Psychological Monographs* 53, no. 2 (Urbana: University of Illinois, 1941), p. 22.

21. *The Problem of Knowledge,* p. 216.

22. *An Essay On Man,* p. 27.

23. Ibid., p. 32.

24. Ibid., p. 24.

25. *The Problem of Knowledge,* Chapter 11.

26. Cassirer, *An Essay On Man,* p. 67.

27. *The Psychology of Learning* (New York, 1913); also *Animal Intelligence* (New York: Macmillan, 1911), pp. 119ff. See *An Essay On Man,* p. 32.

28. "Cassirer's Doctrine of the A Priori," in Schilpp, pp. 175–76.

29. "The Philosophical Anthropology of Ernst Cassirer and Its Significance in Relation to the History of Anthropological Thought," in Schilpp, pp. 495, 514–15.

30. *An Essay On Man,* p. 31.

31. Seymour W. Itzkoff, *Ernst Cassirer: Scientific Knowledge and the Concept of Man* (Notre Dame, Ind.: University of Notre Dame Press, 1971), Chapter 8.

32. See, for example, Noam Chomsky, "Review of B.F. Skinner's 'Verbal Behavior,'" *Language* 35 (January-March, 1959), 26–58.

33. T. Dobzhansky, *Mankind Evolving* (New Haven: Yale University Press, 1962).

34. George G. Simpson, *The Meaning of Evolution* (New Haven: Yale University Press, 1967), pp. 149–150.

35. See Loren Eisley, *The Immense Journey* (New York: Harper, 1957); also Gavin de Beer, *Embryos and Ancestors,* 3rd ed. (Oxford, 1958).

36. Eisley, *The Immense Journey, p. 90.*

37. See, for example, Arthur Koestler, *The Ghost in the Machine* (New York: Macmillan, 1968).

38. "Cassirer, NeoKantianism, and Phenomenology," in Schilpp, pp. 799–854.

39. "Cassirer's Theory of History As Illustrated in His Treatment of Renaissance Thought," in Schilpp, p. 704.

40. "Philosophical Anthropology: The Educational Significance of Ernst Cassirer" in *Cultural Foundations of Education* (New York: Harper & Brothers, 1957), p. 301.

41. Ibid., p. 297.

42. "Ernst Cassirer's Philosophy of Culture," in Schilpp, p. 573.

43. Ibid., pp. 573–74.

44. Kaufmann, "Cassirer, Neo-Kantianism, and Phenomenology," in Schilpp, p. 840.

45. Ibid., p. 841.

46. Ibid.

47. Ibid., pp. 833–34.

48. Ibid., p. 843.

49. Ibid., pp. 844-45.

50. "Kant and the Problem of Metaphysics," trans. by Moltke Gram, in Moltke Gram, *Kant: Disputed Questions* (Chicago: Quadrangle Books, 1967).

51. *"Spirit" and "Life" in Contemporary Philosophy*, translated by Robert W. Bretall and P.A. Schilpp, in Schilpp pp. 857–880.

52. Langer, "On Cassirer's Theory of Language and Myth," in Schilpp, p. 399.

53. Ibid., p. 398.

54. *The Myth of the State,* p. 37.
55. Ibid.
56. Ibid., p. 43.
57. Ibid., p. 373.
58. Ibid., p. 374.
59. See this volume, p. 113.
60. *"The Myth of the State",* p. 375.

Chapter Six

1. See for example, Charles Coulston Gillispie, *The Edge of Objectivity* (Princeton: Princeton University Press, 1960).
2. Pos, "Recollections of Ernst Cassirer," in Schilpp, p. 67.
3. Ibid.
4. Ibid., pp. 68–69.
5. Ibid., p. 69.
6. *Social Thought in America* (Boston: Beacon Press, 1957).
7. *The Myth of the State,* p. 375.
8. See for example Susanne K. Langer, *Philosophy in a New Key* (Cambridge: Harvard University Press, 1942) and *Feeling and Form* (New York: Scribner, 1953).
9. Cassirer, *An Essay On Man,* pp. 144–45.

Selected Bibliography

BIBLIOGRAPHY

HAMBURG, CARL H., and SOLMITZ, WALTER M., comp. "Bibliography of the writings of Ernst Cassirer." In *The Philosophy of Ernst Cassirer,* edited by Paul Arthur Schilpp, pp. 883–910. New York: Tudor, 1949.

KLIBANSKY, RAYMOND, and SOLMITZ, WALTER. "Bibliography of Ernst Cassirer's Writings." In *Philosophy and History: The Ernst Cassirer Festschrift,* edited by Raymond Kilbansky and H. J. Paton, pp. 338–53. New York: Harper Torchbook, 1963.

PRIMARY SOURCES
1. Major Systemic Works

Substance and Function (1910) and *Einstein's Theory of Relativity* (1921) (published in one volume). Translated by William C. Swabey and Marie Collins Swabey. New York: Dover Publications, 1953.

The Philosophy of Symbolic Forms. 3 volumes (1923, 1925, 1929). Translated by Ralph Manheim. New Haven: Yale University Press, 1953, 1955, 1957.

Language and Myth (1925). Translated by Susanne Langer. New York: Dover Publications, 1953.

Determinism and Indeterminism in Modern Physics (1936). Translated by O.T. Benfey. New Haven: Yale University Press, 1956.

The Logic of the Humanities (1942). Translated by Clarence Smith Howe. New Haven: Yale University Press, 1961.

An Essay On Man (1944). New Haven: Yale University Press, 1944.

The Myth of the State (1945). New Haven: Yale University Press, 1946.

2. Major Historical Works

Leibniz' System in seinen wissenschaftlichen Grundlagen (1902). Includes *Descartes' Kritik* (1899). Georg Olms Verlagsbuchhandlung, 1962.

Das Erkenntnisproblem in der Philosophie und Wissenschaft der neueren Zeit. Vols. 1–3. Berlin: Bruno Cassirer, 1906, 1907, 1920; Vol. 4. Stuttgart: W. Kohlhammer, 1957. Volume 4 published as *The Problem of Knowledge* (New Haven: Yale University Press, 1950).

193

Freiheit und Form (1916). Darmstadt: Wissenschaftl. Buchgessellschaft, 1961.

Kant's Leben und Lehre. 2nd ed. Berlin: Bruno Cassirer. 1921.

The Individual and the Cosmos in Renaissance Philosophy (1928). Translated by Mario Domandi. New York: Harper, 1964.

The Philosophy of the Enlightenment (1932). Translated by F.C.A. Koelln and J.P. Pettegrove. Boston: Beacon Press, 1955.

The Platonic Renaissance in England (1932). Translated by J.P. Pettegrove. Austin: University of Texas, 1953.

*Descartes. Lehre, Persönlichkeit, Wirkung.*Stockholm: Bermann-Fischer Verlag, 1939.

The Question of Jean-Jacques Rousseau (1932). Translated by Peter Gay. New York: Columbia University Press, 1954.

Rousseau, Kant, and Goethe: Two Essays (1945). Translated by J. Gutmann, P.O. Kirsteller, and J.H. Randall, Jr. New York: Harper, 1963.

SECONDARY SOURCES

1. Analytical Studies

CASSIRER, TONI. *Aus meinem Leben mit Ernst Cassirer.* New York: Privately issued, 1950. The autobiography of Cassirer's widow places the philosopher in the context of central European intellectual and cultural life amidst a panorama of historically important personages. The autobiography makes no attempt at an in depth study of the man or his philosophy. Nevertheless, it is worth translating and publishing for the flavor of the times.

HAMBURG, CARL H. *Symbol and Reality: Studies in the Philosophy of Ernst Cassirer.* The Hague: Martinus Nijhoff, 1956. This is a series of studies of Cassirer's symbol concept as it relates to other contemporary philosophical positions. The approach is to the logical status of symbolic knowledge and is particularly appropriate for comparative analysis.

ITZKOFF, SEYMOUR W. *Ernst Cassirer: Scientific Knowledge and the Concept of Man.* Notre Dame: University of Notre Dame Press, 1971. This is a study of Cassirer's developing understanding of the status of scientific knowledge and its ultimate revelation of the paradoxical nature of human thought. The author outlines the implication of Cassirer's concept of *animal symbolicum* for an evolutionary interpretation of man and the impossibility of obtaining "objective" knowledge.

KLIBANSKY, RAYMOND, and PATON, H. J. eds. *Philosophy and History: The Ernst Cassirer Festschrift.* New York: Harper Torchbooks, 1963.

These essays are unrelated to but inspired by Cassirer's historical work. It features such thinkers as Johan Huizinga, Leon Brunschwicg, Etienne Gilson, Erwin Panofsky. This is a truly significant collection capped by a topical bibliography of Cassirer's writings.

SCHILPP, PAUL A., ed. *The Philosophy of Ernst Cassirer.* New York: Tudor, 1944. Here is a classic Library of Living Philosophers collection of critiques of Cassirer's philosophy. The volume is introduced by a biographical essay and is concluded with an English rendering of Cassirer's *Spirit and Life.* Cassirer died before he could reply to these critiques.

2. Reviews: The following reviews represent several more insightful analyses of Cassirer's ideas:

EMMET, DOROTHY. Review of *The Philosophy of Ernst Cassirer,* ed. P.A. Schilpp. In *Mind* 59 (1950), 256-261.

HALLOWELL, A. IRVING. Review of *The Philosophy of Ernst Cassirer,* ed. P.A. Schilpp. In *American Anthropologist* 52 (1950), 96-99.

JENKINS, IREDELL. Review of *The Philosophy of Ernst Cassirer,* ed. P.A. Schilpp. In *Journal of Philosophy* 47, (1950), 43-55.

KAUFMANN, FRITZ. Review of *An Essay On Man.* In *Philosophy and Phenomenological Research* 8 (1947-48), 283-287.

NAGEL, ERNEST. Review of *The Problem of Knowledge,* Vol. IV. In *Journal of Philosophy* 48 (1951), 147-151.

Index

196